THE MAKING OF CHA

British Politics and Society

ISSN 1467-1441

Series Editor: Peter Catterall
Institute of Contemporary British History, London

Reflecting a belief that social and political structures cannot be understood either in isolation from each other or from the historical processes which form them, this series will examine the forces which have shaped contemporary British politics and society. Social change impacts not just upon voting behaviour and party identity, but also the formulation of policy. But how do social changes and political developments interact? Which shapes which? Books in the series will aim to make a contribution both to existing fields, such as politics, sociology or media studies, as well as opening out new and hitherto neglected fields such as management history.

The Making of Channel 4 is the first in this new series.

Institute of Contemporary British History

ICBH

The Institute of Contemporary British History was founded in September 1986 to stimulate research into and analysis of recent history, through conferences, publications, and archives and other research tools, which will be of value to decision-makers, students and the wider public. It aims to be both a centre of excellence for research into recent British history and a source for advice and information for researchers and those with a general interest in the field.

The Making of Channel 4

Editor

PETER CATTERALL

Institute of Contemporary British History
and
Queen Mary and Westfield College, University London

FRANK CASS
LONDON • PORTLAND, OR

First published in 1999 in Great Britain by
FRANK CASS PUBLISHERS
Newbury House, 900 Eastern Avenue, London IG2 7HH

and in the United States of America by
FRANK CASS PUBLISHERS
c/o ISBS, 5804 N.E. Hassalo Street
Portland, OR 97213-3644

Website www.frankcass.com

Copyright © 1999 Frank Cass & Co. Ltd.

British Library Cataloguing in Publication Data

The making of Channel 4
1. Channel Four Television Company 2. Television broadcasting
– Great Britain – History
I. Catterall, Peter, 1961–
384.5'54'0941

ISBN 0 7146 4926 0 (cloth)
ISBN 0 7146 4485 4 (paper)
ISSN 1467-1441 (British Politics and Society Series)

Library of Congress Cataloging-in-Publication Data:

The making of Channel 4 / edited by Peter Catterall.
    p.   cm.
Includes bibliographical references and index.
ISBN 0-7146-4926-0. – ISBN 0-7146-4485-4
1. Channel Four (Great Britain)–History. 2. Independent
Broadcasting Authority–History. I. Catterall, Peter, 1961– .
HE8700.9.G7M35 1998
384.55'06'541–dc21   98-29722
                                                                  CIP

All rights reserved. No part of this publication may be reproduced, stored in or introduced into a retrieval system, or transmitted, in any form or by any means, electronic, mechanical, photocopying, recording or otherwise, without the prior written permission of the publisher of this book.

Printed in Great Britain by
Antony Rowe Ltd., Chippenham, Wiltshire.

Contents

Abbreviations		vii
Chronology		ix
Foreword	**Anthony Smith**	xi
Introduction	**Peter Catterall**	xv
Controversies in the Early History of Channel 4	**Edmund Dell**	1
Channel 4: A View from Within	**John Ranelagh**	53
Establishing the Regulatory Framework of Channel 4	**Shirley Littler**	60
A Defence of the Independent Broadcasting Authority	**Lord Thomson of Monifieth**	75
WITNESS SEMINAR The Origins of Channel 4	(editor) **Peter Catterall**	79
Channel 4: News and Current Affairs 1981–87	**Liz Forgan**	116
Channel 4: The Educational Output 1981–89	**Naomi Sargant**	134
Notes on Contributors		162
Index		165

Abbreviations

ABS	Association of Broadcasting Staff
ACTT	Association of Cinematograph, Television and Allied Technicians
AUSS	Assistant Under-Secretary of State
BAFTA	British Academy of Film and Television Arts
BARB	British Audience Research Bureau
BBC	British Broadcasting Corporation
BFI	British Film Institute
C3	Channel 3 (formerly ITV)
C4	Channel 4
DBS	Direct Broadcasting by Satellite
DTI	Department of Trade and Industry
IBA	Independent Broadcasting Authority
IBT	International Broadcasting Trust
ILR	Independent Local Radio
IPA	Independent Producers Association
ISBA	Incorporated Society of British Advertisers
ITA	Independent Television Authority
ITC	Independent Television Commission
ITCA	Independent Television Companies Association
ITN	Independent Television News
ITV	independent television
LWT	London Weekend Television (ITV company)
MMC	Monopolies and Mergers Commission
NAR	net advertising revenue
OBA	Open Broadcasting Authority
Offer	Office of Electricity Regulation

Ofgas	Office of Gas Trading
Oftel	Office of Telecommunications
Ofwat	Office of Water Services
OU	Open University
PPS	Programme Policy Statement
RPI	Retail Price Index
RTS	Royal Television Society
S4C	*Sianel Pedwar Cymru*
SDP	Social Democratic Party
STV	Scottish Television (ITV company)
ToR	Terms of Reference
TSW	Television South West (ITV company which lost its franchise in 1991)
TUC	Trades Unions Congress
TV-AM	the company which won the initial commercial breakfast franchise and began transmission in February 1983
TVS	Television South (ITV company which lost its franchise in 1991)
WFCA	Welsh Fourth Channel Authority

Chronology

1954 Television Act allows the establishment of commercial television and an Independent Television Authority as regulator.

1955 ITV begins broadcasting.

1961 Pilkington Report published.

1971 ITA statement on the idea of a fourth channel published in December.

1972 Anthony Smith publishes article in *The Guardian* advocating that a publishing channel be established.

1973 First independent radio broadcasts, with ITA becoming IBA to reflect broadened remit.

In May the Minister of Posts and Communications calls for views on the allocation of a fourth channel and possible developments in the distribution of television by cable.

1977 Annan Committee recommends the establishment of an Open Broadcasting Authority.

1980 Broadcasting Act establishes Channel 4. Terms of reference and the Programme Policy Statement are drawn up and promulgated by the IBA in December.

1982   On 2 November Channel 4 comes on air.

Controversy over *Questions of Leadership* begins (ending in 1984).

1985   Littler review of relations between Channel 4 and IBA.

1986   Peacock Report recommends that Channel 4 be able to sell its own advertising.

Controversy over *Greece: The Hidden War*.

1990   Broadcasting Act establishes Channel 4 as a statutory corporation responsible for selling its own advertising.

Foreword

ANTHONY SMITH

Today it is difficult to retrieve the precise feeling of frustration that many television programme makers and would-be makers were experiencing during the early 1970s. Both the transmission of television and the creation of the content were locked up inside two institutions, the BBC and the IBA, who spoke and behaved as if their jointly held monopoly was theirs by a kind of divine right. They operated in the name of the nation, but increasingly it was felt that they had come to serve their own institutional requirements, which were influenced by internal political divisions and career paths. The end product of the broadcasting process had become the continued existence of these organisations. They were very good organisations indeed, but their existence as a duopoly meant that no-one who was not employed by them could ever find expression in these two media of radio and television.

The 'duopoly' as it came to be called had no technological necessity behind it. As the mutual competition of BBC and ITV intensified and as the moving image came to dominate the transactions of politics (as well as everything else) the duopoly came more and more to seem to be a morally unacceptable fact of life. There was a fourth channel which was available in terms of transmission slots, but unused, and ever since the Pilkington investigation of the early 1960s its allocation had been under discussion. In the early 1970s the then Postmaster-General, Christopher Chataway, appeared to be about to allocate it to the commercial television companies of ITV for the sake of 'fairness' (since the BBC had two channels and they had only one between them). This appalling decision, if it had been taken, would have locked British television into the duopoly for ever (or so it then seemed). That threat triggered off between 1970 and 1980 a fierce public debate about the future of the vacant channel. Some television people began to look for an alternative model of broadcasting organisation which could act as a politically viable alternative to 'ITV-2', and my 1972 *Guardian* article emerged from these discussions. Until the actual founding of Channel 4 as we know it today, the plan then sketched out for an Open Broadcasting Authority (OBA) became one of the most widely supported models, but the *Guardian* helpfully allowed me to re-publish the article in their columns in different forms over the years to reflect changing ideas as the debate proceeded.

It was a thrill when the Channel actually began because, in the hands of Jeremy Isaacs – an ITV-2 supporter who came over to the OBA idea – virtually everything one had dreamt the fourth channel might do actually came about. Channel 4 embodied the spirit of the 1972 OBA idea and improved upon it. The new Channel envisaged itself as a national asset. It behaved as if it did not own itself. Its mission was simply the search for talent, the giving of opportunities and the funding of them. Its purpose was to read the needs of the society it served and to give expression to them. My retrospective euphoria is not a later nostalgic construct. I remember feeling every day in the years of formation of Channel 4 that we had really taken hold of a closed thing and opened it up, and in so doing were renewing the culture of the nation. Those who were around at the time might recall those depressing Thatcherist years and might, like me, remember how the programmes of Channel 4, the rows it engendered, the emotions it appealed to, stood out against the prevailing gloom and unhappiness of the time. At first the press jeered at the gaucheries of often quite inexperienced programme makers – and they jeered also because they have never learned to offer praise – but within a few months they had grasped the idea of Channel 4 and criticised it in appropriate ways.

But what about the Channel today? I do feel that it has continued to live up to what was intended, but it has passed into the hands of people who are not primarily inspired by the founding idea of a television channel of which the resources are available to everyone. They observe the 'remit' as it is spelled out in the relevant statutes, but it does not appear to act as their basic motivation. They are of necessity embroiled in the multi-channel competition of the late 1990s, and their programme choices seem to be directed much more at winning audiences than in scrutinising the nation for fresh ideas and talents.

Foreword

I do not mean to criticise them too severely, for their problems are different and the job they do is a good one. But I do mourn the fact that young people find it so extremely hard to get an idea accepted by a commissioning editor. I regret that the senior executives stay working at Channel 4 for far too many years – it was originally intended that the key staff should turn over and return to other parts of the industry after serving a few years on the Channel. And perhaps the competitive situation is forcing the decision-making process too far up the hierarchy. Commissioning editors should get out and about and not work as if they were just another bit of the broadcasting industry. Among its many other benefits the Channel should offer the world a model of simple, open, unencumbered and speedy decision-taking on whether or not to take a programme proposal, while offering informed encouragement to the rejected.

The Channel existed for several years with no more than 200 people on its staff. Today, of course, there has to be an advertising force since the Channel now sells its own commercial airtime, but is the whole of the Channel's bureaucracy really necessary? And that awful building in Pimlico bulging with chromium self-importance? I shudder as I pass. That so many of the Channel's programmes are really good is not the point: we always knew, despite the surrounding scepticism, that there was, and is, enough talent in this country to fill several more channels. What I deplore is the lack of real experiment, the kind of programmes that are hard to watch on the screen unless you realise that they have been inspired by someone – perhaps with little experience – trying to do something and say something different. I am sorry that Channel 4's great well of experimentation on the air seems to have dried up and I do fear that if so little is taken from that well then the next generation of programme makers will be less diverse than they could be. Everyone needs protected space in which to make mistakes and I wish that in this sense the Channel would return to its brief.

ANTHONY SMITH
Magdalen College, Oxford
April 1999

Introduction

PETER CATTERALL

The Institute of Contemporary British History was founded in 1986. Since then one of its distinctive contributions to the study of history has been through the holding of what we call witness seminars. Witness seminars are gatherings of those closely involved in a key event or process in the recent past. They thus represent a distinctive form of oral history, but one in which the interlocutors are not historians armed with tape recorders but former colleagues, whose recollections of what was significant, or even of what happened, may differ from person to person. The object is to cross-check the influences and personalities of the episodes under scrutiny, supplementing the documentary record through a structured conversation with the key participants.

This process can, as in the case of the witness seminar held on Channel 4 in 1994, furnish an opportunity for a many-sided approach to the issues involved, offering the perspectives of the various actors (and some major bystanders) on the debates that marked its early years. By the time this particular seminar was held the ICBH already had a considerable track-record in holding events of this kind. Early witness seminars examined subjects such as the fall of the Heath government, the Winter of Discontent, or the British decision to withdraw from East of Suez. Witness seminars, however, have not just been gatherings of the great and good. Subjects have also included the 1936 Battle of Cable Street and the British participants in the International Brigade during the Spanish Civil War. The role of the media has been explored in witness seminars on controversial programmes such as *Yesterday's Men* (broadcast in 1971) or *Real Lives* (1985).

The witness seminar on Channel 4 held at the Institute of

Historical Research in London on 8 June 1994 was, however, not only to discuss a number of the controversial programmes that marked the early years of the Channel and to revisit the internal debates of the time over programme commissioning, content and quality. Another key theme of the seminar was the relationships the new channel had with the Independent Broadcasting Authority, with the existing ITV companies, and with the independent television producers. The first was formally Channel 4's parent, and also its regulator. The ITV companies were suppliers of some of its programmes and sold Channel 4's advertising time, but were also, in time, potential competitors for advertising revenue. The independents, meanwhile, had high hopes that Channel 4 was going to be their channel, and an outlet for their programmes.

The new fourth channel had been a matter of controversy for some years before it even came on air in 1982. Quite what shape it should take was a matter of discussion throughout the 1970s. Many of the participants in the seminar had been closely involved in this process, in the IBA, the ITV companies, the independent sector or the Home Office (which was then the responsible ministry), while others had been not entirely disinterested observers at the BBC. The result was a channel of mixed parentage. These origins very much shaped the early years of Channel 4. Each group – the IBA, the ITV companies and the independents – had their own expectations of the new channel.

No less significant was the funding regime established for the new channel. Not only was it set up to cater for those tastes not currently catered for by the existing ITV coverage. Experimentation was also encouraged by the fact that there were no direct pressures to build an audience, since it was not Channel 4 but the ITV companies who had to sell its advertising space. At the same time there was the pent-up demand for a new and broader outlet for broadcasting ideas which the advent of Channel 4 released and partly satisfied. The result when broadcast was an eclectic mixture which, initially at least, was often of very uneven quality. It did not build an audience through an evening in the way the existing three channels sought to do, nor was it constrained to by financial exigencies. Indeed, to some extent the way the new channel began was almost antithetical to such notions. The very flat management structure that Channel 4 began with was designed to facilitate the autonomy and innovation of each commissioning editor; what it did not facilitate was co-ordination

Introduction

between them. The result, however, was not just days of widely diverse programming. Encouraged by the nature of some of the demand they were seeking to satisfy, though reflecting as well no doubt the political predilections of some of the commissioning staff, the result could be periods when everything the Channel showed, no matter who the target audience purportedly was, seemed to adopt the same tone or subject. Greenham Common, for instance, could feature as a stock item on a range of programmes. Individually this might be justified, but over several programmes the effect could become cumulative and grating.

Edmund Dell, the Channel's first chairman, certainly could find it so. The result was a number of battles fought with the Chief Executive, Jeremy Isaacs, over some of the work being broadcast. Dell's concern, however, was not just over the quality of the Channel's output, but the nature of its relationship with the IBA and the ITV companies. This became even more of an issue with the publication of the Peacock Report in 1986. Peacock reported in favour of terminating the existing financial arrangements between Channel 4 and ITV and recommended that the Channel be allowed to sell its own advertising time and become financially independent. Dell's conviction that this was the right way forward was not, however, shared even by many on his Board, and it was to be another decade before Peacock's recommendation was implemented in full.

It was Edmund Dell who was the key moving spirit behind the witness seminar held in 1994, an edited and annotated transcript of which now appears for the first time. This seminar was an opportunity to revisit the Dell-Isaacs years at the Channel in the 1980s, which saw the Channel born, vilified, and then gradually establish an audience and a profile, as well as the enactment of the struggles mentioned above. Hitherto only Isaacs had told his side of the story in the autobiographical *Storm over 4*. Now Dell offered his memoirs of the period in a piece specially drafted for this seminar, which is reproduced here. This is not only a response to Isaacs, a battle which was rejoined in the seminar (as one participant told me afterwards, 'It was just like that at Channel 4 Board meetings'). It is also a discussion of the idea of regulatory capture; that the responsible authority, the IBA, was so solicitous of the interests of the ITV companies it purportedly regulated that this had a marked and in Dell's view deleterious effect on its approach to Channel 4.

The Making of Channel 4

Given the vision of Channel 4 Dell pursued, made clear in his paper, this view is not surprising. But it is also not surprising that others, especially those with IBA connections, did not share this view. Dell's paper, circulated to all participants before the witness seminar, therefore drew a variety of responses. Shirley Littler offers a rather different perspective from Dell in the paper reproduced here, from someone who was closely involved in the legislative process that led to the establishment of the Channel as a civil servant in the Home Office, and who later moved on to a leading position in the IBA. Lord Thomson of Monifieth, who was unable to attend the seminar, was then her chairman. He, however, offered in response to Dell an account from the IBA side of its relations with Channel 4.

The other responses reproduced here come from three of the Channel's first commissioning editors (and first employees), Liz Forgan, Naomi Sargant and John Ranelagh, none of whom were able to attend the seminar. Their accounts cast light on the commissioning process in what was then a very new situation, a broadcaster acting as a publisher rather than as a producer, and on the innovatory interpretations of their briefs used, for instance by Naomi Sargant, in expanding the understanding of educational television. In the process Channel 4 came to address subjects and audiences which had certainly not been catered for before on ITV. It encouraged a trend towards more short-run commissioning for more specialist audiences. And it challenged existing notions of impartiality on television which proved controversial both at Board level and in negotiations with the IBA.

Objectivity for the historian is as elusive as it proved for many of Channel 4's early programmes. Where some of these programmes erred was in presenting only one side of the story. As these various witness accounts show, there are many. Therefore, that participants remember and emphasise different things does not prove that one is right and the others wrong. Instead, in a sense, they are all telling their own stories, reflecting their particular perspectives, knowledge and objectives. These objectives in particular were grounds for differences between the various players in this scene. In the early years the fledgling channel was subject to the interests of its assorted sponsors. It constituted, at least in the world of British television, a radical experiment which allowed new and sometimes very discordant voices onto the screen. Strong personalities such as Dell and Isaacs had firmly-held and to some extent opposed visions of how the new

Introduction

channel would develop. The very creation of a channel which was primarily a publisher of other people's material, and therefore an outlet which had not previously existed, was itself bound to create diverse expectations. The accounts in this book therefore offer a range of views on what this channel was for.

Particular thanks must go to Edmund Dell, without whose suggestion and encouragement none of this would have happened. Thanks must also go to all of the participants and contributors, many of whom were patiently assisting me in my attempts to elucidate and annotate the transcript of the seminar years after the event actually took place, to Paul Nicholson who took the recording and to Anne-Marie Weitzel, who transcribed the witness seminar. Finally, though by no means least, thanks must go to Channel 4 itself, for its generous contribution towards the cost of transcribing and editing the witness seminar and for permission to reproduce the Channel 4 logo on the cover.

Controversies in the Early History of Channel Four

EDMUND DELL

Prehistory

I distinguish the early history from the prehistory of Channel 4.[1]

The prehistory of Channel 4 is well documented. There was a long debate on how the UK's fourth terrestrial television channel should be used. ITV wanted it as their equivalent of BBC2. The Annan Committee, reporting in 1977, recommended an Open Broadcasting Authority (OBA) which would act as a publisher of programme material provided by the ITV companies and by 'a variety of independent producers' who would be encouraged to 'say something new in new ways'. One question was how the new channel would be funded. The obvious answer was by advertising, but the Treasury, with reason, was afraid that an OBA would need some government funding as back up. Many of those most active in the campaign for Channel 4 saw it as a counterbalance politically to what they perceived as the right-wing bias of the existing media. It was generally agreed that Channel 4 should present a distinctive voice though what exactly that meant depended on who was speaking at the time. Among the most influential voices in this debate was Anthony Smith, now President of Magdalen College, Oxford, who had given evidence to the Annan Committee and who was to become a member of the founding Board of Channel 4. As Secretary of State for Trade in the Callaghan government I was a member of the Cabinet Committee which considered the Annan Report. Nevertheless I played no part in this debate mainly because I was hardly aware that there was a

---

Edmund Dell, Chairman of Channel 4, 1980–87.

1

question. There were enough experts on the committee, particularly Bill Rodgers and Tony Benn, and I had other things to do. It never occurred to me that I would ever have responsibility for the fourth channel.

The debate was eventually settled by William Whitelaw, who became Home Secretary in 1979. His solution, incorporated in the Broadcasting Act 1980, was for a Channel 4 company to be established as a subsidiary of the Independent Broadcasting Authority [IBA] and funded by a subscription levied on the ITV companies which, in return, would sell Channel 4's advertising time. The only sacrifice the Treasury had to make was to agree that the subscription should be taken into account in calculating the levy paid by the ITV companies in recognition of their monopoly of commercial television advertising. The sacrifice imposed upon the ITV companies was to have lost the opportunity of having their own equivalent of BBC2 and to be presented with a bill, for the funding of Channel 4, the size of which, in 1980, was impossible to calculate. Whitelaw, in an offhand reference which greatly annoyed Sir Brian Young, Director General of the IBA and another strong formative influence on the creation of Channel 4, commented that Channel 4 could not expect indefinitely to be a charge on ITV. Whitelaw's warning may have been well judged. But there was no time limit in the legislation.

While the Broadcasting Bill was making its way through Parliament I was, in February 1980, invited by Lady Plowden, Chairman of the IBA, to become chairman of a committee of 'consultants' which would, pending enactment, commence the task of setting up the Channel 4 company and would become its first Board when the Bill became law. It would be a part-time appointment. It would involve two days a week during the preliminary phase setting up the Channel 4 Company. Thereafter it would involve only one day a week. Lady Plowden assured me that the creation of Channel 4 was the last big challenge in television. Inspired by her assurance, I accepted her invitation with an enthusiasm undimmed by an entire ignorance of what the chairmanship would involve. I understand that my appointment had the approval of Whitelaw. The committee of consultants included four representatives of the ITV companies upon whom it had fallen to fund Channel 4. Three of them were Managing Directors. Despite any reservations they might have had about the Whitelaw solution, and its implications for their companies, they could

Controversies in the Early History

not have been more helpful in the early days of Channel 4 though, inevitably, they had conflicts of interest. A major example occurred whenever the Channel 4 Board discussed its subscription application to the Authority. They handled this conflict of interest entirely correctly by explaining the views of their companies, which was helpful, but abstaining when decisions had to be taken on such matters. Problems could also arise when, for example, in the early days of *Channel 4 News*, they wanted to protect ITN from the wrath of many of their colleagues on the Channel 4 Board.

Jeremy Isaacs has it that when I was invited to become chairman of Channel 4, I did not own a TV set.[2] This story had wide circulation within the television industry. It is amusing but not quite true. I had bought my first TV set in April 1979, ten months before Lady Plowden's visit. It is true that my mind was not clouded with much knowledge about television and that I did not know personally or even by name any of those whose important function it is to produce TV programmes rather than present them. Thus my nomination was a typical British amateur appointment but I would not entirely rule out the possibility that the IBA was right in its choice in the peculiar circumstances of Channel 4.

Setting up the Channel 4 Company

The early months were occupied with the legal work involved in setting up the company, finding it accommodation, and numerous other tasks specific to the formation of a television company of a new kind. During this period, the committee of consultants was greatly helped by Ken Blyth, whose normal tasks were to assist the Director General of the IBA. In addition there were two fundamental tasks which would in many ways determine the future of the channel. The first was to regulate relations with the IBA. With Lady Plowden in the chair this caused little difficulty. The second was to find a Chief Executive. Ignorant as I was of the television community, I did not realise that, in their eyes, he had already been found and was simply waiting confirmation that his aspiration was to be satisfied.

Regulating Relations with the IBA

Terms of Reference [ToR], written in dry technical words, were agreed with the IBA. But the Board, influenced particularly by Tony Smith, felt that there should be, in addition, an inspirational Programme Policy Statement [PPS]. The IBA agreed, produced a draft and presented it to the Channel 4 Board for its comments. The ToR and the PPS were promulgated by the IBA at the same time as, in December 1980, the consultants were formally converted into the Channel 4 Board. The word 'remit' is often used in relation to Channel 4. The word refers to the special programming responsibilities of Channel 4, the defence of which has motivated much debate on the future of Channel 4 in a climate becoming hostile to idealistic ambitions. It is the PPS that embodies the remit. The PPS stated that Channel 4 had 'as a particular charge the service of special interests and concerns for which television has until now lacked adequate time. The Fourth Channel is expected, by providing a favoured place for the untried, to foster the new and experimental in television.' Channel 4 was intended 'to complement and to be complemented by the present ITV service.' The PPS added: 'The additional hours of broadcasting made available by the Fourth Channel increase opportunities for programmes directed to different kinds of minority groups within the community, whether ethnic, cultural, or occupational distinctions mark them off from their neighbours.' The PPS underlined the role of the independent sector in helping to achieve these goals. It was clear from the PPS that making mistakes in the interests of innovation was a permissible risk for the new channel.

Appointment of the Chief Executive

The Board decided that the executive team should be headed by a Chief Executive. As Channel 4 was to be a programme company, the Chief Executive should be a programme person. I received many letters telling me that the indicated person for the task was Jeremy Isaacs. I read many articles in the newspapers to the same effect. It may be that the expectation that Isaacs would be appointed persuaded some qualified candidates not to apply. One clearly qualified candidate who did not apply was Brian Wenham, regarded as a highly successful controller of BBC2. The Board considered whether to invite Wenham to apply but decided not to do so on the grounds that he had probably made a career decision leading to Director General of the BBC. Years later Wenham applied to be Jeremy's successor. If Wenham had put his name forward the first time round he might well have been appointed and he might have become Director General of the BBC.[3] Other non-applicants *were* approached. One was Brian Tesler, Managing Director of LWT. He had made a considerable impression on me as one of the group of consultants which became the Channel 4 Board. He preferred to stay at LWT.

Isaacs had indicated his strong interest in becoming the first Chief Executive of the new channel in the MacTaggart lecture which he had delivered at the Edinburgh Television Festival the year before. His lecture has been described as 'the most eloquent and public job application in the history of television'. I, however, have been quoted as follows:

> There are two things in that lecture that I didn't particularly like. I knew nothing about television, but what I did know was that there wasn't much on television that I actually liked, and therefore I wanted it to be different. Jeremy told me two things in the MacTaggart Lecture: different but not too different, and ITV2 not Channel Four. Now to me the key things were, Channel Four, because that was symbolic and the second is that I did want it to be distinctive. So as far as I was concerned the MacTaggart lecture was dissuasive not persuasive.[4]

Three candidates made it to the final short list. Paul Bonner had impressed the Board at his first interview but clearly did not consider himself qualified for such a job and frankly told the Board so. The Board agreed while feeling, nevertheless, that Bonner might well have a role to play in the future of Channel 4. Isaacs, at both interviews, gave the laid back performance of a man who knew, as it turned out rightly, that the job was already in his pocket. The outstanding candidate, both at the first and second interviews, was John Birt. He had been recommended to me by John Freeman, Chairman of LWT. He had worked hard at his application. He had very clear ideas for the future of Channel 4 which he had developed in a 50-page submission.

However my colleagues on the Board, much more knowledgeable than I, warned me that, under Birt, Channel 4 would be too serious and that he had never yet held an appointment even as senior as that of Programme Controller at LWT. It was felt that to appoint Birt was too great a risk. On the other hand the Board also felt that there were risks of a different kind with Isaacs. It was decided to appoint Isaacs but to invite him to find a senior programme position for Bonner. After discussion with Isaacs, Bonner accepted appointment to a role described as 'Channel Controller' without a seat on the Channel 4 Board though he attended it *ex officio*.

From these events arose two resentments. Jeremy became aware that his chairman had had strong doubts about his appointment, and he resented the fact that Bonner had been imposed on him.

Jeremy's resentment increased when, a little later, the IBA, concerned at the lack of balance in Channel 4's early current affairs output, appointed Bonner to the Channel 4 Board in the hope that, with the enhanced status of an executive director, he could exercise a moderating influence. I accepted the decision though without too much confidence in the outcome.

Getting on Air

There were 26 months between September 1980 when Jeremy was appointed, and 2 November 1982 when Channel 4 came on air. This was little enough time for preparation. During this period many decisions had to be made and corners cut. A Board normally meeting formally once a month was bound to feel excluded from many decisions that it considered important and debatable. But there was no other way and, despite some criticism from some members of the Board, that was the way that, in those early days, things had to be done. During this period there was only one hiccup in my strengthening relationship with Jeremy: the appointment, without consultation with me, of Liz Forgan as Senior Commissioning Editor for News and Current Affairs. Jeremy records, this time accurately, his response to a question from me at his final interview. My question was how, in his view, a chief executive should relate to a chairman. His reply was: 'He should keep him informed of anything of moment, consult him and seek to carry him with him in any major matter.' There could be no doubt that the appointment of the Senior Commissioning Editor for News and Current Affairs was a major matter but I had not been consulted. In his book Jeremy is sarcastic about what he describes as my wish to appoint as current affairs commissioning editor a cross between the editor of the *Financial Times* and a Harvard economics professor.[5] I accept the spirit of this criticism. I was never entirely happy with Channel 4's current affairs output, and *Channel 4 News* began very badly. This was a continuing source of disagreement between us. I made sure that no appointment of such seniority within Channel 4 was ever made again without the agreement of the Board. With that important exception, my own feeling was that relations between chairman and Chief Executive became mutually supportive during this period of preparation. Even Jeremy recalls that at the moment on 2 November 1982 when the TV screen lit up and Channel 4 came on air for the first time we were sitting together in his office and he lent across and shook my hand.[6]

The early days of Channel 4 on air were fraught. Audiences were small. The tabloid press attacked the channel for being boring. The right-wing press attacked the channel for its left-wing bias. The ITV members of the Board were seriously worried. If Channel 4 went on as it began, whence could they expect to recoup their money?

Who would advertise on such a channel? The welcome moment of relief from this mountain of criticism, at least some of it justified, came with the beginning of TV-AM in February 1983. It appeared that TV-AM was even worse than Channel 4. The tabloids switched their target. Channel 4 was left in relative peace while the famous five fought for survival. Channel 4, having survived these early months, went on to achieve both a *succes d'estime* and, in my view, commercial viability. Indeed its success became a danger to the BBC. The tabloid press saw in the success of Channel 4 an opportunity to whip the BBC. As usual in such circumstances, the pendulum swung from one extreme to the other. Channel 4 started by being unable, in tabloid eyes, to do anything right. It ended by being unable, in tabloid eyes, to do anything wrong.

I experienced one moment of moral hazard. A Conservative MP told me that he did not agree with the criticism of Channel 4. A channel that was prepared to broadcast Wagner's *Ring of the Nibelungs* deserved praise not criticism. I hesitated. Could I afford to lose a single friend? I then confessed that the Ring was being broadcast not on Channel 4 but on BBC2.

The Issues

Channel 4 being launched, what were the issues during the remainder of my chairmanship which ended on 30 June 1987? I select for discussion the following among the many that arose:

- 'Due impartiality'

- Relations with the IBA, which I found to illustrate the phenomenon of regulatory capture

- Following the Peacock Committee Report – should Channel 4 fund itself by selling its own advertising time?

On 'due impartiality' I was, I think, at most times at one with the IBA, and the issue led to tension between the chairman and Chief Executive and, indeed, between the Chief Executive and the Board. The tensions that arose became public. I had the impression that someone at Channel 4 was briefing his friends in the press against me. On the first anniversary of Channel 4, 2 November 1983, there was one particularly unpleasant attack on me in the press. Hardly had I read it when Jeremy rang to invite me to a small dinner to celebrate the anniversary.

On the other hand, relations with the IBA became ever more difficult and led to a series of confrontations. My impression was that on these issues I had the support, sometimes reluctant, of the Chief Executive. These problems did not become public at the time. I did not think that it was in the interest of Channel 4, or for that matter the IBA, that they should become public. Much of the material under this head in this essay has never previously been made public.

On whether, following the Peacock Committee Report, Channel 4 should support the switch to selling its own advertising time, I was alone, opposed by the IBA and by the whole of the Channel 4 Board apart from Lord Blake. Here publicity was inevitable. I had to defend my position publicly, the more so as I was in very much of a minority in commercial television circles.

I do not here consider those other Channel 4 programmes which might be considered as expressing the remit. I could not watch the whole of Channel 4's output. My viewing was highly selective. Some programmes I enjoyed. Many I was quite incapable of appreciating. I thought the 'Film on Four' series masterminded by David Rose was, in general, admirable and a credit to Channel 4. Sometimes I felt that some films, not from the David Rose stable, were being shown more to startle and to prove that Channel 4 had the courage to do what no other channel had dared to do than because of any intrinsic merit. Jeremy would say of such films that only ten people had complained but that a million had enjoyed them. But there was no evidence that anyone had enjoyed them and sometimes such evidence as we had suggested that no one had enjoyed them. However, these programmes seldom raised issues which divided me from my Chief Executive. So I do not discuss them here.

'Due Impartiality'

Television channels were rightly required by law to show due impartiality. Channel 4, however, had a prehistory which made this more difficult. Many of its principal advocates saw Channel 4 as the Left's opportunity to balance the right-wing slant of the rest of the media. There were those who told me that objectivity was a false ideal. All it meant was acceptance of establishment attitudes which Channel 4 should be challenging. Too many of the Channel's commissioning editors appeared to share this point of view. It was rather naive considering that the channel had been set up by a Conservative government. My view was that this was not a position that it would be right or tenable for Channel 4 to adopt. It would not be right because Channel 4, as a national channel using a scarce resource, could not be governed by the wishes of a small group of left-wing idealists. It was not tenable because the law governed Channel 4 as well as ITV and the law had to be respected. By respecting the law Channel 4 would disappoint many who had fought for it. But the duty was inescapable. Channel 4 was not required to balance every programme. But Channel 4's output as a whole had to be balanced. My principal fear from the appointment of Jeremy as Chief Executive had been that the channel would not show due impartiality. In my conversations with him before Channel 4 came on air I insisted on due impartiality from the beginning and this he readily accepted. On this there was no apparent difference between us. But, in the early days, as subsequently admitted by Jeremy among others, Channel 4 had a left-wing bias. Criticism on that score was well founded. I found this seriously worrying and was not alone in that view.

Whitelaw raised the problem with the IBA and also complained personally to me. Tony Smith raised the question of bias at the Board. The excuse given was that left-wing producers were easier to find than right-wing producers. I considered this excuse unacceptable. At the Edinburgh Television Festival of 1983, Jeremy admitted the problem so far as to announce his intention to find more right-wing journalists. The intention was right but I found the method odd and, indeed, it epitomised the problem of bias on the channel with which the Board was confronted. Whatever his personal point of view, a good journalist or producer should be able to produce a balanced programme. Apparently those we were commissioning could not or did not see the need.

Jeremy summarises my attitude as follows:

> Edmund Dell had high expectations of the intellectual quality of television journalism, never having seen anything of it before being appointed to Channel 4. He was gravely disappointed – appalled is probably more accurate – by what he found. He had, he said, no overriding political objection to the work he most despised; it was simply that it was not good enough. Put that right, and any associated political problems would vanish. Not only that, he was of the view that high quality journalism would be an important means of increasing our audiences, though a quick comparison between the circulation figures of the *Financial Times* and of other newspapers might have disabused him of that.[7]

I have no wish to dissent from what he says apart from the snide remark about my never having seen television journalism before being appointed to Channel 4. I may not have had a TV set until April 1979 but, like other MPs, I did watch television news and current affairs especially when they bore on my departmental responsibilities as a Minister. Jeremy notes that, although by law Channel 4 was compelled to have regard to due impartiality, I was much more concerned with quality than with balance. It was a point I made to him so often that it would have been difficult for him to forget it. I did believe that higher standards would help significantly with the problem of due impartiality. Whether I was right on the point of audience building was never tested. With time Channel 4 did accumulate larger audiences, several times touching Jeremy's target of 10 per cent in his time as Chief Executive. The problem was that these audiences were built by American imports and by the soap opera *Brookside* rather than by those programmes which embodied the Channel 4 remit. Who can say that higher quality current affairs might not have won larger audiences? Jeremy was sure that they would not and he may have been right. It is a pity that there was no experiment of that kind.

The most significant point, however, about this quotation from Jeremy's book is its implicit, and complacent, recognition that Channel 4's current affairs programmes were not very good. This went with a conviction on his part that it did not matter very much and that Channel 4 did not really have to make a greater effort. Apparently, in his view, Channel 4 could not afford high quality current affairs even though it did not have to earn its own living, at least in the short term. This was, for me, a bitter disappointment. Whenever I had been asked during the preparatory period what would be different about Channel 4, I had emphasised the opportunity we had for raising the quality of current affairs programmes on television.

There were some reports that, during this difficult initial period, the Board considered sacking Jeremy. This is not true. Brian Tesler, at the first weekend seminar that the Board held three months after coming on air, did express considerable concern at the reputation the channel was acquiring with the public. But there was no suggestion that the Chief Executive should resign. During one heated discussion between Jeremy and me about due impartiality he did ask me whether I was seeking his resignation. I replied that I was not. The problem as I saw it was to correct the channel's political steer and to raise the quality of its current affairs output, not to sack the Chief Executive.

Although considerable power was delegated to the Chief Executive, the Board was ultimately responsible for programming. It was understood that commissions of probable sensitivity should come to the Board before contracts were signed. The Board regularly debated programme output. I discuss here a number of specific issues that were illustrative of the problem of due impartiality and which were considered by the Board:

- The Friday Alternative
- IBT
- Questions of leadership
- Greece: The Hidden War

The Friday Alternative

The view of many of those who had campaigned for Channel 4 was that TV news, whether from ITN or the BBC, had a right-wing bias. The idea therefore arose that there should be an alternative news programme. This 'alternative' was produced by an independent, Diverse Productions. It appeared on Channel 4 each Friday evening for half an hour, cutting the time available for *Channel 4 News* on that evening to half an hour. I did not consider this experiment with an 'alternative' news a success. The problem was not so much that it was consistently left wing as that it was consistently poor. Nevertheless Jeremy recommended that the series should continue after its existing run came to an end. The Board was divided with the ITV representatives on this occasion strongly on my side but with other influential voices taking the view that Channel 4 should persist with the experiment. After a long discussion, Jeremy agreed to bring forward a revised proposal. *The Friday Alternative* was replaced by another series from Diverse Productions entitled *Diverse Reports*. This series gradually improved and eventually became a much better and more balanced contribution to Channel 4's current affairs output. Another consequence was that, in due course, *Channel 4 News* was extended to 50 minutes on Friday evenings as well. A leading spirit at Diverse Productions was David Graham who had left the BBC to set up this new independent company. Some of the television producers who set up their own companies found in managing them a new experience which influenced their outlook on life. Rather later, David Graham was to produce for Channel 4 the right-wing series *The New Enlightenment*. He was also to become one of those who decided, after the Peacock Committee Report, that Channel 4 should sell its own advertising time. Some commissioning editors at Channel 4 also began to appreciate, as the 1980s progressed, that there were political ideas other than left-wing ideas.

IBT

The International Broadcasting Trust was established by worthy people including Judith Hart. They hoped to produce for Channel 4 programmes about the developing world. As they had some money they could help to fund them, not an unimportant consideration. The problems of the developing world were certainly fit material for Channel 4. But, like other political and economic problems, there existed then as now a diversity of views about appropriate policy for the developing world. IBT had only one view. Moreover the programmes were in no way distinctive and merely repeated at greater length the simplistic and sentimental approach to developing country problems

Controversies in the Early History

that regularly appeared on the other TV channels. They were also very poor of their kind. I could have no objection to the IBT view being presented on Channel 4, though preferably with rather more sophistication. But the IBT series left no room for other views. My opinion was that, in commissioning the series, Jeremy had departed from the principles of Channel 4. He had succumbed to political pressure from a lobby and to a desire to avoid controversy with the Left who were expecting Channel 4 to be an outlet for their propaganda. In his book Jeremy confesses that the IBT programmes showed an 'apparent proselytizing intention' adding that the programmes 'were not that bad, but they were not very good'.[8] He claims that no one else offered to provide a series about the developing world. This excuse is nonsense. Channel 4 commissions were valuable. Approaches could have been made to other possible providers and a very much better series could have been commissioned. It was easier to give in to pressure.

Questions of Leadership

The ITV company, Central Television, was commissioned to produce one, perhaps two, one hour programmes about trade union leaders. The brilliant film and television director, Ken Loach, was to produce them. Given his well known political views, there could be no dubiety about the nature of the programmes that would be offered to Channel 4. In fact Central offered four programmes and they severely criticised Frank Chapple and Eric Hammond of the electricians union and Terry Duffy of the engineering union. Chapple and Duffy were offered an opportunity to appear in a discussion programme after the end of the series but both refused and, indeed, threatened legal action for defamation. There could be no certainty that such an action would not succeed. Their refusal to appear was understandable. After, as they saw it, being traduced for four hours, they would then be confronted by their accuser and would share with him a discussion programme on the issues he had raised. Why should they bother, thereby implicitly legitimising the programmes? This was an example of a continuing problem with Channel 4's current affairs. Programmes were produced whose bias was only too easy to forecast. But no plans were made in advance to produce balancing material. In this case there were two additional factors. More programmes had been produced than had been authorised by Jeremy. Moreover, despite Loach's justifiable reputation, they were intolerably boring. They would turn Channel 4's audiences away in droves. All this raised some questions of principle which I debated in public with Loach who, not unexpectedly, was dissatisfied with my arguments.

I was not opposed to Channel 4 publishing the Loach programmes provided they were shortened and a balancing programme was associated with them. I was not, in that context, prepared to accept that the refusal of persons criticised to appear to answer criticism should be a bar to publication. On this basis, with the support of the Board, the programmes were returned to Central to be remade into two programmes with some balancing material. I would then have been prepared to take the risk of an action for defamation. But as others clearly were not prepared, in the light of the legal advice, to take that risk, I argued long and hard with Terry Duffy and Frank Chapple, both of whom I knew, that they should withdraw the threat of legal action. I told them that it was ludicrous to imagine that such programmes would in any way damage them. I persuaded Duffy so far as to get from him an assurance that he might be prepared to withdraw the threat of legal action if Chapple would also withdraw. Chapple told me that he would be prepared to think further about the matter but that he would first like an opportunity, with Eric Hammond, to see the two programme version privately. I warned him that I would not expect him to be better pleased by the new version than with the old. But he appeared amenable to my persuasions. I had reason to think that by this time he was beginning to realise that his reputation would be more damaged by his threat of legal action than by the publication of the programmes.

Although the IBA had not given its formal approval to the broadcasting of the revised programmes, there was reason to think that it was now happy from the point of view of balance. But by this time the public controversy had led the Central Board to demand a viewing of the programmes produced under their auspices. They were shocked by them, and also still frightened by the threat of action for defamation.[9] They decided that they would not return them to Channel 4 in any form. I did my best to persuade the Central Chairman, Sir Gordon Hobday, to let Chapple and Hammond see the two-programme version. I told him that we could then see 'whether it would be possible to take this matter further on the basis that the trade union leaders concerned withdraw their threat of legal action and that,

Controversies in the Early History

in return, we create an opportunity for them to reply on television in whatever reasonable manner they think fit.' Offering people criticised an opportunity to see programmes in advance raised serious questions of principle. I could only make the suggestion in this case because, at an earlier stage of the dispute, Central had already offered Chapple an opportunity to view in advance. I had no success with Hobday. The programmes were never shown on Channel 4 and, in view of the attitude of the Central Board, Channel 4 did not have to pay for them.

The incident with *Questions of Leadership* had a salutary effect on the Channel 4 commissioning process. A committee was established under Liz Forgan to look ahead and plan where balancing material would clearly be necessary. This did not always work but, gradually, the situation improved.

Greece: The Hidden War

It is worthy of some comment that Channel 4 did not have problems of this kind exclusively with independent producers. Channel 4 had as much difficulty with ITV companies. A series about the Greek civil wars after the liberation from German occupation was produced for Channel 4 by TVS in 1986. This series led to complaints from distinguished British citizens who had been involved in Greece at the time. They had been interviewed for the series and now accused Channel 4 both of bias and of misrepresentation. The Board asked Jeremy to enquire personally into the matter. He did so and came to the conclusion first that in many respects the complaints were justified and secondly that Channel 4 should return to the subject in order to restore balance to Channel 4's coverage of the historical issues raised. This conclusion was reported to the complainants most of whom were satisfied that Channel 4 had dealt with the matter fully and honourably. Nevertheless it was of some concern that, as late as 1986, what Jeremy describes as 'a series of mistakes that cost us dear' should have been made.[10] It showed that Channel 4's systems were still not foolproof.

Complaints had also been made to the IBA. The IBA also accepted that Channel 4 had dealt with the matter appropriately. There was, however, something more to be learnt from this incident and I pointed it out to the IBA. The only reason that this series had led to complaints was the involvement of distinguished British citizens. But the whole time seriously unbalanced programmes about foreign countries were appearing on commercial television and the IBA did nothing about it. Apparently due impartiality only applied to such programmes if they involved British citizens. Thus, for example, Channel 4 could be found presenting programmes about Grenada and Mozambique which, in the light of subsequent events, can be seen to have been nothing but propaganda. The IBA, however, was not interested. It was only on exceptional occasions that I could vet such programmes. Therefore my own interventions had to be limited to criticism after the event. One of my proposals, which came to nothing, was that we should appoint David Watt, about to retire as Director of Chatham House, as our current affairs consultant on a part time basis. I did eventually, in my last year as Chairman, persuade Jeremy that Channel 4 should establish, on an experimental basis, an advisory committee on current affairs. I hoped, by these proposals, to show him that even television producers and commissioning editors might have something to learn from those whose everyday life brought them into contact with the great current affairs issues and that the problem between us was not just my unwillingness to be satisfied. It was no use my insisting on either David Watt or my current affairs advisory group before Jeremy was ready to accept the idea. To have done so would have resulted in frustration for David Watt and would merely have wasted the time of the excellent people we recruited to the committee which operated under my chairmanship. How useful the committee was must be a matter of judgement. Its life was not continued after my departure and after Jeremy had been turned down as Director General of the BBC.

Relations with the IBA or Regulatory Capture

The phenomenon whereby the regulator is captured by those he is appointed to regulate is well known and extensively studied. Probably in no field of human activity is such capture more likely than in television. Television people, by and large, are attractive, articulate, interesting, and dedicated. Moreover they are able to advance the claim for which there is much justification though, from another point of view, it is to damn with faint praise, that British television is the best in the world. Why therefore interfere? If it ain't broke, why fix it? In the UK there was the division between the BBC, funded by the licence fee, and ITV funded by advertising. The BBC governors are the BBC and are ultimately responsible for it. The IBA's function was to regulate

Controversies in the Early History

commercial television and to be ultimately responsible for it. The genius of British commercial television, it was held, the reason it had not gone down market as many critics, including George Thomson, had earlier forecast, was the combination of regulation and the monopoly in television advertising that ITV enjoyed. As they did not have to compete for television advertising they had no need to go down market. The typical ITV executive was as devoted to public service broadcasting as his BBC competitor. There was much truth in this but it did not mean that everything that was going on in British commercial television was defensible and in the public interest. I was half amused, half worried by the love match between the IBA and ITV. For the IBA, commercial television was theirs. The IBA thought it its duty to defend ITV against the BBC, the government, and against critics. They came to see their function as more to defend than to regulate. The language used by the IBA was the language of the friend, sometimes the candid friend, not the language of the regulator on behalf of the public interest. Some of that language will be found quoted in this essay. Only at licensing time did the IBA show its virility by sacking some existing licensees, usually for reasons obscure to the outside observer. The relationship was celebrated on social occasions when there was much mutual back slapping. It was all only too understandable but it was not the object of the regulatory exercise. Compare the IBA as a regulator with Oftel, Ofgas, Ofwat and Offer.

There were, in fact, many issues on which the IBA should, in the public interest, have been taking a tough line with the ITV companies but it did not. I mention a few:

- Poor industrial relations in ITV led to high costs at the expense of the viewer. This was mainly the fault of management. Management's excuse usually was that the ITV companies had bravely faced one strike, had been defeated, and it had cost a great deal of money. Hours of broadcasting lost could never be recaptured. It was better to give in. The inflationary effect of this permissive attitude spread across television. It made life harder for the BBC with its constrained licence fee. It put up production costs and, so far as Channel 4 was concerned, reduced the real value of the subscription.

- The ITV companies had a monopoly of television advertising. In recognition of this fact they paid a levy to the Treasury. The

Treasury wanted more, the ITV companies wanted to pay less. The levy was based on profits. The problem with the levy as it existed was that it resulted in a high marginal rate of taxation on the ITV companies, thereby encouraging waste. The Peacock Committee Report showed how net advertising revenue had risen without any corresponding increase in the levy.[11] It expressed its concern at 'the severe weakening of incentives for cutting costs'. This was a situation in which the IBA should have been an impartial arbiter on behalf of the public. In fact it saw its function as being to defend the ITV companies from the Treasury. The Authority saw no evidence that the high marginal rate of tax had acted as a deterrent to cost consciousness.

A possible solution to the conundrum was to base the levy on revenue rather than on profits. The IBA successfully resisted any such outcome to the negotiations that took place.

- Channel 4's success in promoting independent producers as suppliers to Channel 4 was enthusiastically endorsed by the Government. Eventually, in 1986, Douglas Hurd, as Home Secretary, announced that independent producers should supply 25 per cent of the schedule both on the BBC and ITV. The Peacock Committee had suggested 40 per cent but this was more than could reasonably be expected at that time even as a target. I welcomed this development even though it could make life harder for Channel 4 by increasing the negotiating strength of independent producers by giving them alternative outlets for their work. The IBA vigorously opposed it on behalf of the ITV companies.[12]

- Perhaps the most obviously ludicrous aspect of the dichotomy between the BBC and ITV was that the consumer was forced to buy two magazines to find the week's programmes. But it was an arrangement which the ITV companies found profitable. Instead of being on the side of the public interest and seeking a way of ending this absurd situation, the IBA did all it could to preserve it. The problem was referred to the Monopolies and Mergers Commission [MMC]. The IBA was delighted when the MMC, by a narrow majority, supported the *status quo* thereby proving that even that prestigious institution could sometimes forget that it was there to serve the public, not vested interests.

Controversies in the Early History

For Channel 4, the IBA's relaxed attitude to its regulatory duties led to various unfortunate results:

(1) The IBA had arranged that Channel 4's signal should go through the ITV companies where the advertisements would be inserted. This was totally unnecessary technically. It made Channel 4 the victim of ITV's poor industrial relations. It was not until the end of 1984 that the IBA agreed that, in the event of emergencies such as industrial disputes, the Channel 4 signal could be transmitted independently of the ITV companies.

(2) Because the Channel 4 signal went through the ITV companies, any extension of Channel 4 hours of broadcasting required agreement with the ITV unions which did not have the policy of giving much for nothing. Moreover any increase in Channel 4 hours of broadcasting could add to the numbers of ITV staffs and represent for the ITV companies an increase in costs irrespective of the outcome of trade union negotiations. This was a significant handicap to Channel 4 and led to many delays in expanding Channel 4 hours.

(3) The ITV companies were also concerned at what they described as the balance between supply and demand of advertising time. Any increase in Channel 4 hours implied an increase in advertising time and hence could soften the advertising market. ITV's concerns on this matter were, for them, entirely legitimate though one expert, Harold Lind, prepared a paper, commissioned by Channel 4, in which he argued that the launch of Channel 4 had not softened ITV advertising rates and that a further increase in Channel 4 broadcasting hours would not have a significant adverse effect. ITV questioned Lind's conclusions on the grounds, among others, that his results might have been influenced by the IPA/Equity dispute which had for some time distorted the effects of the Channel 4 launch on advertising rates. These were not matters on which entirely uncontroversial conclusions were ever likely to be agreed. The decisive question was to determine where lay the public interest. That was the IBA's responsibility. There was no public interest in managing advertising time with the deliberate purpose of keeping advertising rates high. The IBA should have been much firmer with the ITV companies on this issue. In fact the IBA was much too concerned with ITV's commercial interests.

The Making of Channel 4

(4) Channel 4 wished to know the revenue resulting from the sale of its advertising time month by month. It did receive informal information, particularly from the major companies, by various routes. Thus by the summer of 1984, information suggested that some of the major companies were taking 7 per cent of their advertising revenue on Channel 4. One London company was taking 9 per cent. But Channel 4 wanted the actual figures and considered it absurd that these should be kept confidential from it. It was asking for this information not company by company but as a total. This was already a concession because it was believed in Channel 4 that not all companies were making even a respectable attempt to maximise revenue from Channel 4. It had already been agreed that, in March 1985, over two years after Channel 4 had come on air, separate annual figures would be published a year in arrears. At a liaison meeting with ITCA on 7 February 1985 I emphasised that Channel 4's revenue figures should be public knowledge, that it was important to know how much of the subscription was being covered and the extent to which revenue was related to audience. I was told that Channel 4's revenue figures were irrelevant. The industry was running a two channel system and what counted was the total revenue. ITV was unique in publishing monthly figures of total revenue and was under no obligation to do so. Any suggestion that Parliament might be interested, for example, in how far the levy was being reduced by the cost of the subscription, was swept aside. It had nothing to do with Parliament. The fact that the levy was being reduced did not mean that the public was paying anything towards the cost of Channel 4. The discussion ended with the ITCA representatives agreeing to think further about the matter. But it was my view that this was another of the matters in which the IBA should intervene decisively and, while respecting necessary commercial confidentiality, put an end at once to the companies' reticence about an issue that was clearly a matter of public interest.

(5) The IBA had an abiding fear that Channel 4, with increasing success in audience terms, might start arguing in favour of itself selling its own advertising time. If this happened it would be damaging to ITV. It might also, possibly, deprive the IBA of its offspring. The IBA had already lost the Welsh Fourth Channel

Controversies in the Early History

which, in the original Whitelaw Broadcasting Bill, though not in the 1979 Conservative manifesto, was to be part of Channel 4. Gwynfor Evans had persuaded Whitelaw to change his mind back to the Conservative election promise of a separate Welsh Fourth Channel by threatening to fast to death. I thought Whitelaw very sensible to give in to Gwynfor even though, thereby, I lost part of my job. The IBA had fought hard against the change of mind and, having lost S4C as it became, did not wish to be robbed further by losing the parentage of Channel 4. By the time Channel 4 came on air, Lord Thomson had replaced Lady Plowden as chairman of the IBA. The IBA, under Lord Thomson, was very proud of Channel 4. It laid on anniversary champagne breakfasts at which more or less appropriate speeches were made. This possessive attitude towards Channel 4, and defensive attitude on behalf of ITV, led to the problems in the IBA's relationship with Channel 4.

I illustrate the problem of the regulator captured by discussing three issues that arose in relations between the IBA and Channel 4:

- The drama of *Channel 4 News*.
- Channel 4's use of independent producers.
- Evidence for Peacock

The Drama of Channel 4 News

A 50-minute news programme at 7 p.m. was one of Channel 4's innovative ideas. The IBA had strongly encouraged Channel 4 to commission its news programmes from ITN which was owned by the ITV companies. In fact, when Channel 4 started out, there were few if any credible alternative suppliers. Some members of the Channel 4 Board considered that ITN could not supply a distinctive news service suitable for Channel 4 and that it would be better to take risks with others than be safe, but not distinctive, with ITN. After discussion, the Board decided to commission its news service from ITN subject to an explicit condition, stated in the contract, that the news service had to be to the satisfaction of Channel 4. Unfortunately, in the early days, *Channel 4 News* was far from satisfying anyone at Channel 4, let alone Channel 4's viewers. The Channel 4 Board was prepared to accept that a news service of the quality it wanted might well get quite small audiences by the standard of the normal BBC1 and ITN news

The Making of Channel 4

programmes. But we found that we had commissioned a poor programme which was achieving very poor viewing figures.

It was decided that Jeremy and I should meet Lord Buxton, Chairman of ITN, and David Nicholas, Editor of ITN, to express our strong concerns and to establish what ITN intended to do to rescue the situation. In the end we had a series of meetings. Solutions were canvassed to which we were prepared to give approval but subject to the clear understanding that, if ITN failed again, Channel 4 would exercise its rights under the contract and cancel it. To protect the Channel 4 position under the contract I informed Lord Buxton at our final meeting that I would be writing to him to set out Channel 4's position in the matter.

I drafted a letter and showed it to Jeremy who gave his full approval to what I had written. Indeed, throughout this episode, I had the impression that I enjoyed Jeremy's full support as well as of the Board as a whole apart from the ITV representatives who, understandably, had divided loyalties. It was, as it had to be, a strong letter. The letter was then despatched (see Appendix 1). The Director General of the IBA, John Whitney, attended meetings of the ITN Board as an observer. When the ITN Board, consisting of Managing Directors of ITV companies, saw my letter they were distressed. What was the chairman of Channel 4, funded as it was by ITV, doing writing such letters? It was decided, with John Whitney's support, to put the matter to Lord Thomson. At a meeting with him attended also by Jeremy and John Whitney, Lord Thomson demanded that I withdraw the letter. I refused. I think Lord Thomson realised that for me this would be a resigning matter. He did not persist with his demand. There could be no doubt, however, that ITN and the ITV companies would feel under less pressure knowing that they had Lord Thomson's support. I regarded Lord Thomson's attitude as indefensible. The IBA was supposed to regulate ITV, not to protect it from justified criticism and pressure. As a matter of fact, *Channel 4 News* under the leadership of Stewart Purvis did improve and it became possible for the Channel 4 Board to take pride in a programme that although winning small audiences by some standards, nevertheless fulfilled the Channel 4 remit.

Channel 4's Use of Independent Producers.

Apart from *Right to Reply*, Channel 4 did not make its own programmes. It was a publishing house. This was a key difference between Channel 4 on the one hand and the BBC and ITV on the other. There were three possible sources of Channel 4 programmes: programmes commissioned from ITV companies, programmes commissioned from independent producers, and purchases off the shelf, often from the US. Channel 4 was encouraged to commission independent producers. It was part of the Channel 4 remit stated clearly in the PPS. It was thought that independent producers would be able to produce more cheaply and thus force down ITV costs which had been unduly raised by the regular submission of ITV companies to trade union blackmail. The IBA had, in 1980, suggested a rough breakdown which it expected might eventuate as between the different possible sources of supply. It emphasised that the 'overriding concern will be the quality of the programmes'. Subject to that 'prime qualification', it thought that 15–35 per cent of Channel 4's output would come from independent producers, 25–40 per cent from the major ITV contractors, a further 10–20 per cent from the regional ITV contractors, up to 15 per cent from ITN, and 5–14 per cent from foreign sources. As it turned out, independent producers were making good offers to a greater extent than expected and were therefore gaining more commissions than expected. This led the ITV companies to complain to the IBA.

In December 1983 Jeremy and I had our regular budgetary meeting with the IBA. At the meeting Lord Thomson read out a text, a copy of which he handed to me after the meeting. He asked that I write to him if I had any comments. This text, apparently part of a longer document, read as follows:

> At the same time, it is recognised that the independent sector exercises a healthy downward pressure on ITV costs which is in the longer term interests of the companies and is to be encouraged. The IBA recognises, however, that Channel Four, as part of Independent Television, is financed by the ITV system, and that if price and quality are right ITV companies ought to enjoy in terms of planning and commissioning programmes a relationship which reflects their significance to the system as a whole.

This was obviously an ill-considered attempt to influence Channel 4's editorial judgement and to get more programmes commissioned from ITV. The fact that such a draft should have been read out at an official meeting between the Authority and Channel 4 and then handed to me for comment, was deeply worrying as an example of regulatory capture at its worst. I wrote to Lord Thomson on 10 December 1983. I first pointed out that the question touched on by the text he had given me was already dealt with in the PPS in the following terms:

> In achieving an appropriate balance of output, the Fourth Channel will observe a balance between different sources of supply. The Authority welcomes the positive injunction given it by Parliament to encourage the work of independent producers, and will want to have early and regular assurances that this is being done. It will also expect the regional companies within ITV to make a due contribution to the schedules of the Fourth Channel. Through a national network, the Channel should reflect regional diversities.

I went on to point out that if the draft became an instruction from the IBA to Channel 4, it would have to be published, perhaps as an amendment to the PPS. My letter continued:

> The question would then arise as to its exact significance. It can be interpreted as saying nothing much more than one would normally expect from the relationship with ITV that exists. But as it would clearly be a change it would not be seen that way. It would be seen as an instruction from the IBA to the Channel Four Board to commission more from ITV, inevitably at the expense of the independent producers who must now also be regarded as an important part of the commercial television system. I believe that this would produce an unfavourable public reaction.
>
> First it would be seen as protection for the ITV companies whose employment practices are not highly regarded... Secondly I have been greatly impressed by the very positive reaction in Government circles to what we have done to encourage independent production both for its own sake and because of the employment and competition with ITV that it has created... Thirdly the draft will lead to controversy as to what the phrase 'price and quality are right' is intended to mean. A favoured position for ITV, which would inevitably be seen as the implication of the draft, would equally be seen as undermining

Controversies in the Early History

the very positive factor with which the draft begins, that is the competitive effect of the independent sector on ITV costs...

We have done a great deal in Channel Four to co-operate with [ITV] and we are prepared to do more. But to create the impression, or the reality, that in commissioning terms they are being put in an even more favoured position than their considerable production resources should in any case have created for them would not, in my view, be acceptable to public opinion.

It was some time before it became clear whether my arguments had proved persuasive. On 17 January 1984 Lord Thomson replied to my letter. The subject, he said, was 'a sensitive one which, at this stage, needs to be discussed between us as a matter of confidence'. It was, however an issue, 'which needs some attention'. There was a 'widely held and genuine belief amongst the companies that the programme acquisition decisions of Channel 4 have been biased against them'. Subscribers to this view included 'senior figures in ITV whose judgement we would both respect, and who are particularly well disposed to Channel Four'. The indications were that the ITCA companies were 'likely in 1983/4 to account for 37 per cent – within, but very much at the lower end of the indicative range – while the independents are likely to take 52 per cent – well above the top end of their range. The outlook for 1984/5 is that these percentages will remain at much the same levels.' He went on to say that 'it would strike me as odd, given the pressing need for the highest quality programming, if for any length of time the ITCA contribution remained at the rather low levels indicated so far.' The last sentence was particularly surprising to me in view of the IBA's general approval of Channel 4's performance.

The IBA recurred to the matter at liaison meetings between Lord Thomson and myself. An example was the meeting on 27 February 1984. The IBA referred to worry on the ITV side about Channel 4's acquisition policy. There were indications that the proportion of ITV programmes shown on Channel 4 were settling down at a relatively low level. Any justified ITV grievances would adversely affect ITV's attitude to the subscription. It would be helpful if Channel 4 could do something to set ITV fears at rest. But while willing to convey ITV's complaints, the IBA had been warned off any overt *Diktat*. The IBA apparently hoped that Channel 4 would understand its embarrassment and do the decent thing by ITV without actually being instructed to do it. But this was precisely what Channel 4 would not do. The ITV companies had to continue competing on their own merits. But their representatives raised the matter on several occasions at the Channel 4 Board and it was also raised in other fora.

At a meeting of the Channel 4/ITCA Liaison Group on 7 February 1985, ITCA representatives complained of a slight further drift towards independents and asked what message could be taken back to the ITCA Council in view of the fact that not all of them were happy with the current arrangements. The complaints came particularly from the regional companies which had developed the feeling that it was difficult to place product with Channel 4. Both Jeremy and I emphasised that Channel 4 had no policy of allocating quotas for either ITV or the independents. David Plowright, representing ITCA acknowledged that one major advantage stemming from the lower costs of the independents' products had been the opportunity for changes in patterns of work within the ITV companies.

By 1986 the breakdown between the various sources of supply was 43 per cent from independent producers, 39 per cent from ITV and ITN, and 18 per cent spent on feature films and acquired material. At a meeting with the IBA on 11 December 1986, when we were discussing the implications of the Peacock Committee Report, I pointed out that a funding system that led to the expectation that Channel 4 would buy a certain proportion of its schedule from ITV companies blunted the cost reducing influence of Channel 4 purchasing power. I referred to the IBA guidelines on this point. At this point Lord Thomson intervened and said that he thought we realised that we had persuaded the IBA to abandon them. I replied that I had not been aware of it but that, if it were the case, the IBA should announce it publicly. No such public announcement ever took place to my knowledge. Indeed Channel 4 had never been told though its ignorance had not been allowed to influence editorial decisions. The matter was referred to again at a liaison meeting with Lord Thomson on 5 January 1987. John Whitney said that the ITV companies would be told of the IBA's position at a future meeting. Thus it took the IBA four years to inform the ITV companies of its change of position.

Evidence for Peacock

The gravest crisis in the relations between Channel 4 and the IBA arose over the Peacock Report. The IBA suspected that Channel 4 might, in its evidence, recommend that Channel 4 should sell its own advertising time in competition with ITV. Perhaps it was worried by Channel 4's insistence on knowing the value of the revenue invoiced on Channel 4 instead of simply accepting the ITV argument that they were operating a two channel system and all that mattered was the total revenue. Justin Dukes, Managing Director of Channel 4, had made some unauthorised threats of this kind though, when the matter was discussed by the Channel 4 Board after the Peacock Report, he was not among those who supported the idea.[13] There was in fact at the time no danger at all of Channel 4 presenting such evidence to the Peacock Committee. Although relationships between Channel 4 and the IBA had proved less happy than I had hoped and expected in the days of Lady Plowden, I was still opposed to the idea and so was the Board. Lord Thomson, however, thought it right to send me a message in which the third paragraph read as follows:

> While there may be some natural differences of emphasis between the points which the IBA and Channel Four would wish to make to Peacock, in the light of their different responsibilities and experience, I am sure you will understand me when I say that it would be wrong for the evidence given by Channel Four, as the Authority's wholly owned subsidiary, to cut across in any significant way the evidence to be given by the Authority itself.

I was appalled by the suggestion that Channel 4 should not give its honest judgement to a government committee, only that judgement of which the IBA felt able to approve. I did not expect any important difference between the evidence Channel 4 would give and that which the IBA would give. But here was a matter of principle that could not be ignored. Apart from any question of principle there was the practical point that coerced evidence from Channel 4 would be valueless. Channel 4, in my view, must give its evidence freely or not at all.

The Board met on 21 May 1985 and, on my proposal, passed a resolution repudiating the implied instruction from the IBA. The resolution was as follows:

The Board has noted the letter dated 17th May 1985 from the Chairman of the Independent Broadcasting Authority to the Chairman of the Channel Four Television Company Limited regarding the handling of evidence to the Peacock Committee, and in particular the following sentence:

While there may be some natural differences of emphasis between the points which the IBA and Channel Four would wish to make to Peacock, in the light of their different responsibilities and experience, I am sure you will understand me when I say that it would be wrong for the evidence given by Channel 4, as the Authority's wholly owned subsidiary, to cut across in any significant way the evidence to be given by the Authority itself.

If this sentence means that the evidence to be presented by Channel Four has to be approved by the Authority, then the Board puts it on record that, in its view, it has a public duty which requires it, unconstrained by the evidence to be provided by any other body, to give honest and independent evidence to the Peacock Committee, and that this is a duty which cannot be subordinated to the wishes of the Independent Broadcasting Authority.

The Board further resolves that its status as a wholly owned subsidiary of the Independent Broadcasting Authority in no way affects its responsibilities in the performance of this duty.

The Board therefore authorises the Chairman to hold discussions with the Chairman of the Authority with a view to ensuring that the Channel's right to offer independent evidence to the Peacock Committee is clearly understood.

I sent this resolution to Lord Thomson covered by a private letter. This letter read in part as follows:

There are....certain clear principles involved, principles which concern both our public duty and our duty as company directors. These principles require that Channel Four's evidence should be, and be known to be, honest, independent and unconstrained. It must be what the Channel Four Board, not the IBA, wishes it to be. The fact that Channel Four is a wholly owned subsidiary of the Authority is, in this context, irrelevant. Channel Four has, as you acknowledge, different responsibilities and experience, and it must be those that guide its evidence, not pressure from the Authority....

In this matter Channel Four's principal responsibility is to deal openly with the Peacock enquiry, and to give it the best advice we can. Yet now that you have written me a letter which contains a clear threat of possible censorship, with all the appearance of an instruction from the Authority to the Board of Channel Four, it inevitably prejudices the independence of our evidence unless we make the position clear beyond doubt. As Chairman of Channel Four, I am not prepared to see the integrity of any evidence we may give to the Peacock enquiry prejudiced.

There followed a meeting with Lord Thomson after which I was able to send the following message to the Channel 4 Board:

> Evidence to the Peacock Committee. Jeremy and I had a most friendly meeting on Thursday, 23rd May, with Lord Thomson, Chairman of the Authority. David Glencross and Shirley Littler were both present. As a result of the meeting I am satisfied that, after appropriate consultations which will include an exchange of draft evidence both ways between the Authority and Channel Four, Channel Four will be able to give its evidence freely to Peacock. Lord Thomson began the discussion by saying that he had come to the view that the phrase 'wholly owned subsidiary' did not adequately describe the real relationship between the IBA and Channel Four. He thought that, for the future, it was a phrase to be used as little as possible. I accepted his statement with pleasure. A fuller report can be made to the next meeting of the Board. At the meeting with Lord Thomson, he also said that there should be a review, in the light of some years experience, of the ToR.

I could hardly object to that, though I thought it unnecessary. The result of the review was conveyed to us by Shirley Littler, the Director of Administration.[14] In June 1983, she had moved to the IBA from the Home Office where she had been an under secretary concerned with broadcasting policy. What she proposed was totally unacceptable. For example she hinted that possibly 'specific guidance' should be given by the IBA to new non-executive directors of Channel 4 'about the way in which they should approach their responsibilities'. In the light of the recent row about evidence to Peacock which had shown the IBA totally ignorant of the responsibilities of company directors, this was rich indeed. Her paper would have placed Channel 4 under such constraints that it could hardly have issued a press notice without the permission of the IBA. Press statements had not been mentioned in the ToR. Her paper said:

> While Channel 4 must be responsible for its own press statements, it is desirable that they should avoid overt criticism of IBA decisions or attacks on the ITV companies since this could have the effect of weakening the Independent Broadcasting of which Channel 4 is a part....Is it worth agreeing that any press statements by either the IBA or Channel 4 which concern each other should be exchanged before issue?

The tone of the paper generally was totally at variance with the expression of goodwill I had heard from Lord Thomson. At a working dinner on 15 July 1985 with Lord Thomson, John Whitney and Shirley Littler, at which Jeremy and Lord (then Sir Richard) Attenborough were present, I was asked by John Whitney whether, if the IBA persisted, I would resign. I gave them clearly to understand that I would. The Shirley Littler review was forgotten.

The Peacock Committee and the Future of Channel 4

These incidents had their effect on my reaction when the Peacock Committee recommended that Channel 4 should have the option of selling its own advertising time, thus starting a vigorous debate. In some quarters it was suspected that the Peacock Committee had been guided to this recommendation at a lunch which I gave for Alan Peacock.[15] In fact no such idea was put to him at that lunch nor, so far as I know, on any other occasion by anyone connected with Channel 4. Alan Peacock specifically assured me that the idea had not come from anyone at Channel 4.[16] Despite considerable provocation, I was still opposed to the idea and did not change my mind until *after* the Peacock Committee Report.

Paragraph 660 of the Peacock Committee Report said, in part:

> Because Channel 4 is now at a point where its costs are of a similar order to the revenue from advertising we advance:
>
> *Recommendation 14: Channel 4 should be given the option of selling its own advertising time and would then no longer be funded by a subscription from ITV companies.*

The implication of this recommendation is that Channel 4 would no longer be a subsidiary of the IBA. We would, however, still wish to see Channel 4 offering complementary services.

The IBA let me know that they expected Channel 4 to reject this recommendation out of hand. After all, in Channel 4's own evidence to the Peacock Committee, there had been no suggestion of any change to the *status quo* in the matter of the sale of Channel 4's advertising time. I did not see how we could possibly reject this recommendation without consideration. A recommendation had been made and we ought to think about it seriously. The IBA ought to think about it seriously. A majority of the Channel 4 Board agreed that we needed to study the recommendation. Those in favour of a serious study were, as I put it to Lord Thomson in a letter,[17] those 'who have no declarable financial interest in the matter'. The three ITV representatives present expressed their concern but, very properly in the circumstances, did not press the matter to a vote. It was also agreed that, at a Royal Television Society seminar on the Peacock Committee Report, I could give a balanced presentation of the question despite the fact that alarm might be caused by the thought that Channel 4 was prepared to go so far as to study so outrageous a proposition (see Appendix 2). After my presentation, Christopher Bland, Chairman of LWT and former vice-chairman of the IBA, told me that Channel 4's study of the question need take no longer than ten minutes before we rejected it.

My new interest in the subject arose from a variety of circumstances. I no longer had the least confidence in the IBA. To introduce an additional dose of competition into commercial television did not appear to me undesirable provided it did not imperil the Channel 4 remit. Channel 4 now appeared to be earning more than its direct costs. The ITV companies, I suspected, were now making a profit out of the Channel 4 subscription especially when account was taken of their Channel 4 commissions. There was a question about how effectively the ITV companies were selling Channel 4's air time.[18] To them the sale of Channel 4's air time could not be as important as it would be to Channel 4 if Channel 4 was responsible. I was uneasy about how long Channel 4 could really expect to be allowed to spend money that came to it as manna from heaven. Although we had set Channel 4 up to be as economic in its use of its resources as possible, and I had installed every possible protection for the Channel on matters of propriety, I feared that there must be waste.[19] Employment at the channel which had started with an idealistic 100 had now mounted almost to 300. In this fear I was supported by Jeremy who was also concerned that money gifted might not be spent as carefully as money earned. By now I had come to realise that, whatever my own views on programming, Channel 4 was not going to be as up market as I had hoped. Channel 4 was getting its audiences and its share of the market mainly from *Brookside*, a soap opera, and American imports. The programmes that could be defended in terms of the PPS gained only small audiences. If that was to be the character of Channel 4, there really was no reason why it should not earn its own living by selling its own advertising time provided that the remit could be respected at least to the degree that it had so far been respected.

In my mind one further consideration was decisive. With likely changes in the law following the Peacock Committee Report, with increasing, if so far limited, competition from satellite and cable, I feared that a Channel 4 tied by the IBA parentage and the ITV subscription to the interests of ITV would itself be driven ruthlessly down market. In the competitive battle ITV would demand that Channel 4 should be their ally in fighting the competition. Already, to some extent, this had happened. To sharpen ITV's competitive edge by giving it more time for popular programming, Channel 4 had taken from ITV schools programming and horse racing. There would, I forecast, be two stages in Channel 4's decline. In the first it would be the respectable face of commercial television. Its audiences would diminish as it took from ITV all ITV's public service responsibilities and the ITV companies would enjoy the luxury of complaining of the terrible burden Channel 4 represented. In the second phase Channel 4 would be pressured to reduce its own public service programming so as to win audiences for, and therefore advertising revenue for, ITV. An independent Channel 4 selling its own advertising time and therefore free from IBA and ITV pressure now appeared to me the best practical hope of preserving the remit so far as in experience to date it had been respected.

The fundamental question, however, was whether an independent Channel 4 could survive, and preserve its remit, in the more competitive world anticipated. That question now existed in a new context. When considered previously, when Channel 4 had given its evidence to the Peacock Committee, there had existed a possibility that

Controversies in the Early History

the BBC might be funded by advertising at least in part. Now, following the Peacock Committee Report, it appeared that that possibility had been ruled out. What was to be considered now was whether Channel 4 could be viable selling its own advertising time with the BBC still funded by a licence fee. This was a very different context from that which had appeared to exist at the time Channel 4 had given its evidence to Peacock.

As soon as it was heard in ITV that Channel 4 was considering the possibility of an independent existence, threats flowed forth. David Elstein, Programme Controller of Thames, said that if Channel 4 sold its own advertising time, ITV would take it as their first priority to drive Channel 4 out of business.[20] David Shaw, General Secretary of ITCA, issued similar menaces; 'If ITV is forced to compete with Channel 4 then we would hammer it to the ground with our resources.'[21] It seemed to me extraordinary that ITV companies, licensed by the state to make profits from commercial television, should show such arrogance. This language proved that their commercial monopoly had gone to their heads, but it met no rebuke from the IBA or, for that matter, from Parliament. In any case I did not believe it to be true, for two reasons. First, Channel 4 was already receiving via the subscription not less than 13.6 per cent of net advertising revenue [NAR]. It probably would not need much more in order to survive as an independent entity. It would not, I thought, be sensible for ITV to wage war on Channel 4 in the hope of saving a further small fraction of NAR in what would probably be an increasing total. Secondly, the potential competitive strength of Channel 4 appeared to me to be enormous. It was constrained only by the remit. It was the only national terrestrial commercial channel. If ITV forced it to go down market it was more likely that it would be the ITV companies that went out of business not Channel 4. It appeared to me that the ITV companies would have a strong commercial interest in continuing complementary scheduling in order to avoid any down market move by Channel 4. I attempted to persuade Paul Fox, Managing Director of Yorkshire Television and President of the Royal Television Society, then a member of the Channel 4 Board, that complementary scheduling could continue even if Channel 4 sold its own advertising time. I thought I had convinced him but he soon reverted to the self-defeating negative attitude towards the idea of any change being taken up by the IBA and ITV.

The Making of Channel 4

The Board decided to invite Professor Alan Budd, then of the London Business School, to report to it on the prospects for an independent Channel 4. It also invited its auditors, Coopers & Lybrand, to review the Budd report. The name of Alan Budd was suggested by Paul Fox. Budd had helped prepare ITV's evidence to the Peacock Committee and they had been very satisfied with it. Paul Fox hoped, no doubt, to be equally satisfied with his report to the Channel 4 Board. In fact, in his report to the Channel 4 Board in October 1986, Budd conveyed considerable confidence that an independent Channel 4 would be viable. Coopers & Lybrand were, understandably, a great deal more cautious.

Budd's confidence was to some degree justified by information that became available later. In the year to end March 1987, advertising revenue invoiced on Channel 4 exceeded the subscription by about £20 million. However there were certain costs that, under the present structure, Channel 4 itself did not pay. The IBA was threatening that there were all sorts of discretionary charges that could be loaded on to Channel 4 if it was too impudent in its ambitions. These figures, therefore, were not conclusive. It was information in the 1987/88 Report of the IBA that really made the case. It revealed that, for the first time, advertising revenue invoiced on Channel 4 exceeded the estimated total costs of the Channel, and did so by £18.9 million. This occurred even though Channel 4 advertising time was, at the time, being sold by the ITV companies at a discount of 10.3 per cent in the sense that its share of advertising revenue was less than its share of the commercial audience. Professor Alan Budd had examined at length the source of the 'discount' (his term) on the sale of Channel 4 advertising time. He concluded that 'there are good reasons for believing that the relative price of Channel 4's advertising time could be increased if current selling arrangements were changed'.[22] These figures confirmed my view not only that Channel 4 could survive as an independent Authority selling its own advertising time with its remit unimpaired, but that Channel 4 could get more value for its advertising time than the ITV companies appeared capable of doing. Indeed one ITV company managing director of a small ITV company wrote to Jeremy: 'While I know that our Sales Department have always made strenuous efforts to sell both channels I would not dispute that sold on a national basis Channel 4 is likely to take more revenue than at present....'[23]

Controversies in the Early History

These figures also confirmed that the ITV companies, in addition to the monopoly profits they were already making out of their own channel, were now making further monopoly profits out of Channel 4. I could not believe that this was ever the Government's intention.

It was with the assistance of the reports from Budd and Coopers & Lybrand that the Channel 4 Board returned to the subject. The Board was also assisted by a report of an extensive discussion of the issue at the Management Committee on 5 December 1986. I was struck by the conservatism of the Channel 4 management. Only one member seemed to me to come near the realities of the situation faced by the Channel. But it was perhaps inevitable that a management which found itself in the extraordinary position of being allowed to spend a large income which had come to it by way of grant, would not wish to worry about a future in which it might have to earn its way to success. Some strove to have their cake and eat it, preserving the existing scheme while retaining an option to sell separately, the improbable recommendation of Peacock. Thus Paul Bonner wrote to me: '... though I would not dismiss the advantages of selling our own advertising and the implied greater freedom of decision making it would bring, I would only at this stage strive to keep the option of self financing as a possibility.'[24] The conclusions of the management meeting were that if Channel 4 sold its own air time, ITV could regard Channel 4 as its main competitor; that competitive selling was likely to reduce Channel 4 ratings; that Channel 4's share of the commercial audience would therefore fall; and that Channel 4 would probably have to sacrifice the remit in order to remain financially viable.

It rapidly became clear that the great majority of the Board, even those who had thought it right to initiate the Budd and Coopers & Lybrand enquiries, were opposed to Channel 4 independence. The debate took place over several Board meetings. Lord Blake and I argued for independence. Jeremy considered that independence was possible but not desirable. Justin Dukes wanted to preserve the option but not to advocate any change in the current funding arrangements. The remainder of the Board was adamantly opposed. I had hoped for the opportunity of a substantial discussion with the IBA. Although there were a number of private discussions with Lord Thomson at our liaison meetings, at which there was no meeting of minds, the only real discussion on the Peacock Committee Report between myself and the IBA itself took place at a meeting with the Authority on 11 December

1986. Even then we had little time. The Authority was not really interested in a debate with the Channel 4 chairman. They had ITV interests to defend and, in any case, they knew that the division of opinion on the Channel 4 Board favoured my opponents. Lord Thomson reiterated the IBA view. I explained the division of opinion on the Channel 4 Board. I told Lord Thomson that it was now inappropriate that so many members of the Channel 4 Board should have their principal employment in companies standing in a contractual relationship with Channel 4.

I then developed the arguments for an independent Channel 4 which I have already outlined. Jeremy spoke about the difficulties of complementary scheduling if ITV and Channel 4 were competing for advertising revenue. He did, however, add that nevertheless it would not be impossible, it might not even in practice be so very difficult, and that therefore, although he would not advocate independence, he certainly wanted that Channel 4 should have the option and continue to study such questions as to how complementary scheduling could continue.

Lord Thomson said that an independent Channel 4 would need to be franchised. How would that affect the morale of people at Channel 4? I replied that the same question applied to people at ITV whose companies might lose their franchise next time round. In any case the question of whether Channel 4 would need to be franchised would depend on whether an independent Channel 4 was set up as a public company or as a public trust. Lord Thomson wrote to me on 15 December 1986 reiterating the views of the IBA. He thought that competition for advertising between ITV and Channel 4 could not leave complementary scheduling intact. He continued:

> The IBA expects that changes in broadcasting will come about, and is ready to face those changes with realism. At the same time it does not wish to endorse a radical change in the system of funding, the result of which could undermine the strengths and structure of Independent Television, and the service it offers to viewers.

During this period I had the opportunity of two discussions on the subject with Douglas Hurd. One was a private discussion in his office at which I advocated an independent Channel 4. The other was at a dinner in November 1986 to which he gathered a small group of interested people at which again I argued the same case. I do not know how far these discussions influenced the government's decisions. Nor do I know what officials in the Home Office were recommending to their Secretary of State. In Appendix 3 will be found the comments on the eventual White Paper on Broadcasting that I sent to Douglas Hurd, and copied to the Select Committee on Home Affairs, which was reporting on the White Paper. The Select Committee published my views in its Report. But by that time I had long departed from Channel 4.

This controversy was creating such dissension within the Channel 4 Board that I decided that we had to find some way of resolving it which would restore peace without prejudicing the different points of view that had emerged. After all, the debate was about the future and the channel still had to be run and decisions about a multitude of current problems taken. This desire to find a common position was, fortunately, shared and, at our meeting on 18 December 1986, we were able to agree unanimously on the following statement:

> The Channel Four Board is content with the present funding arrangements based on 17 per cent of NAR. If, however, Parliament should wish to alter the structure of broadcasting, the Board would not rule out in advance alternative structures for Channel Four, and would be prepared to discuss such changes on condition that any new arrangements ensured the maintenance of the existing remit.

My kindly intentions in attempting to put the issue to sleep so far as the Channel 4 Board was concerned were immediately exploited by ITV. It was clearly understood at the Board that this statement was without prejudice to any individual member's opinions, including those of the chairman. Nevertheless, David Shaw, General Secretary of ITCA, took it upon himself to state at a *Financial Times* conference on 18 February 1987 that 'The Channel Four Board has unanimously rejected the proposal.' Samuel Brittan, who had been a member of the Peacock Committee, and who was speaking at the same conference, phoned me to ask whether David Shaw had stated the position correctly. I then authorised him, in his own speech to the conference, to say that he had my authority to state categorically that my views were unchanged and that Channel 4 should sell its own advertising time.

So far as the IBA was concerned, I believe that this was the last straw.[25]

I Leave but Continue the Battle

My successor Sir Richard Attenborough who, for most of the seven years of my chairmanship, had been my deputy, was in most respects better qualified than I to be chairman of Channel 4. Indeed I believe he had been offered the post before me and had turned it down only because the making of his film *Gandhi* would not allow him the time [but see p.93]. Now, I thought, the IBA has persuaded him to succeed me because, although he still does not really have the time, at least he agrees with them in opposing independence for Channel 4. It was he who told me that he had been invited to succeed me but, he said, he was still trying to persuade Lord Thomson to extend my own appointment. His attempts were, understandably, unsuccessful and it was announced in March 1987 that he would succeed me from 1 July 1987. Attenborough wrote me a kind letter on 23 March 1987 to which I replied on 25 March 1987.

> It was kind of you to write. I think that there is only one point on which I need comment. I strongly believe you to be wrong about independence for Channel 4.
>
> The arguments against Channel 4 independence are conventional and not thought through. If they succeed, as I suspect they may, they will leave Channel 4 exposed to every change in ITV economics and political expediency. The safest position for Channel 4 is to have its own funding derived from advertising revenue and not to be dependent on the goodwill of the IBA (which has become little more than a servant of ITV interests), ITV, or indeed the Government.
>
> I do not know what the Government proposes to do or whether it will be re-elected to do it. However if Channel 4 opposes this change, and the Government, re-elected, does opt for it, it will have no influence on the manner in which it is done. I note how on the issue of 'independents' the IBA is already being pushed miserably, and without credit, along a road which they should have adopted enthusiastically as soon as Peacock came out.
>
> These words are my testament to my successor.

Controversies in the Early History

With the advantage of being out of the chair, I began to argue against the assumption that there could be no change in Channel 4's status or funding until the end of the present ITV contracts on 31 December 1992. There was, I felt, one important step that could be taken as soon as Parliament had passed the necessary legislation. Channel 4 could be established as a separate Authority on the model of the Welsh Fourth Channel. The Welsh Fourth Channel was a separate Authority, funded in the same way as Channel 4. There was no reason, I claimed, why Channel 4 should not be placed in the same position. It would hardly be reasonable for Channel 4 to have to prepare to compete with ITV in the sale of its advertising time under the aegis of an IBA that opposed such a change and with ITV representatives still on its Board.

This idea would have brought several advantages. First, it would have given Channel 4 time to prepare for the independence, in funding as in other matters, which a re-elected Conservative government was likely to enact. Secondly, it would have enabled Channel 4 to negotiate freely with the ITV companies a subscription which reflected more satisfactorily the actual advertising revenue earned in its advertising time. In that connection, it would have enabled Channel 4 to insist that instead of being given just an annual figure of advertising revenue invoiced, it should have the monthly figures which were at that time being kept from it by the ITV companies. Thirdly, it would have helped to end lingering suspicions among independent producers that the ITV companies had, as funders and suppliers, a privileged foot in the door.

In this small campaign I was unsuccessful. Whatever the government may have thought of the idea, legislative time is always scarce. The change I proposed would have required legislation and the idea of a special Broadcasting Bill for this limited purpose would, no doubt, have exhausted the patience of the government's business managers. However the main point, a Channel 4 free of ITV influence and in a greatly strengthened position as against any continuing regulatory authority for commercial television, was being won.

By early 1989 the IBA had experienced a belated conversion to the proposition that Channel 4 should sell its own advertising time. However, with a myopia that defied belief, it proposed that Channel 4, while selling its own advertising time, should become a subsidiary of the IBA's successor body, the Independent Television Commission

The Making of Channel 4

(ITC). If I had not had my own long experience of the IBA, I would have found it impossible to credit that such a proposal could be seriously contemplated even though it appeared tentatively as one option for the future of Channel 4 in the Broadcasting White Paper. My attempt to deal seriously with the proposition in the White Paper can be read in Appendix 3. But, in fact, it was not an option to be considered seriously. It would have meant that a subsidiary of the ITC was selling advertising time in competition with the Channel 3 companies that the ITC had franchised and was regulating. It would have involved major conflicts of interest. That was understood by the Peacock Committee. That committee, in recommending that Channel 4 should have the option of selling its own advertising time, stated clearly that this must mean that Channel 4 could no longer be a subsidiary of the franchising and regulatory authority for the commercial television industry. The only conceivable reason for such a proposition was that the ITC could thereby blunt Channel 4's competitiveness. Even on its death bed the IBA could not manage to put the public interest before the ambitions of its staff who hoped to move to the new ITC and those of its ITV clients. In the end, the government, still too much influenced by the IBA, nevertheless refused this advice, making Channel 4 a statutory corporation licensed by the ITC but at least not a subsidiary of the ITC.

I was deeply distressed at the way the Channel 4 Board, under Sir Richard Attenborough, handled the discussion with the government leading up to the Broadcasting Act 1990.

On 9 June 1989 I wrote to Attenborough:

> I have deliberately not bothered you with my views about the future of Channel 4.
>
> I know that yours have been very different from mine. In any case it is probably already too late partly owing to the misguided position taken up again and again by the Channel 4 Board.
>
> But last night, when we had a brief chat, you said that an independent trust was the worst possible outcome for Channel 4. Do you really imagine that, with the type of television tycoon who is going to emerge from the tender process, they are going to let Channel 4 alone if they are required to guarantee its income? Do you really imagine that the ITC will protect you? Channel 4 is not going to be living in the era of the estimable Paul Foxes and

Brian Teslers and Bill Browns who love public service television and have had a monopoly to protect their profits and their consciences.

I write more for the record than because I think you will be ready to do anything about it. I told you two years ago that you were profoundly mistaken on this issue. I have not changed my mind any more than, evidently, you have changed yours.

The worst mistake made by the Channel 4 Board was in asking the government for a guarantee of the 14 per cent of net advertising revenue (NAR) which, they calculated, they needed to run the channel. I warned Attenborough that he would have to pay a high price for any such guarantee. In a letter to me of 27 June 1989 he appeared to believe that Channel 4 was going to be guaranteed the full 14 per cent. In fact all Douglas Hurd had said was that if Channel 4's revenue fell below 14 per cent of NAR, ITV was to be required to make it up to the extent of 2 per cent. The rest Channel 4 would have to earn for itself. As the price for this meagre guarantee, if Channel 4's revenue rose above 14 per cent, the surplus would have to be shared with ITV.

I was strongly opposed to the idea of this guarantee. On 26 June 1989 I wrote to Douglas Hurd:

> Thank you for arranging that I be sent a copy of your statement to the House on the future of commercial television. As, since the Peacock Committee Report, I have been an advocate of a Channel 4 trust with sovereignty over the sale of its own advertising time, I welcome your decision to establish such a trust.
>
> The guarantee you propose raises far fewer problems than it would have done in the form recommended by the present Channel 4 Board and the IBA. Nevertheless I believe, given the inevitable uncertainties, that operating on percentages of terrestrial net advertising revenues could well turn out to be inappropriate and this is, therefore, an additional reason why I continue to prefer my own proposal for supplementary assistance to Channel 4.
>
> I write, however, not to question that part of your statement but in the hope that you will reconsider your intention that half of any 'surplus' Channel 4 revenues above a 14 per cent baseline

should be paid to C3. I do not know your opinion on how likely this is to occur. But you would hardly have laid down this provision if you thought it highly unlikely. I believe this provision to be wrong in principle and in practice.

I can see that this arrangement might be regarded as some compensation to C3 for the guarantee. But no compensation should be required. The justification for any assistance from C3 to Channel 4 lies in Channel 4's obligation to preserve its remit rather than release its full competitive power against C3. This is greatly in C3's interest. That alone provides C3 with more than adequate compensation for the assistance it will be required to give.

As a matter of practice, it could lead, if Channel 4 achieves a revenue comparable with its present share of the commercial audience, to a continuing flow of money from Channel 4 to C3, which would be anomalous to say the least. The sums of money involved, while probably small as compared with the revenues of the major C3 companies, could become a not insignificant element in the profits of some C3 companies. It is, therefore, an arrangement that is likely to muddy the relationships between C3 and Channel 4.

I hope that you will reconsider this element in your proposals.

Hurd refused to change the arrangement. He told me in reply that it would strengthen relations between Channel 4 and ITV. The consequence of the arrangement was that, in respect of its first year of operation as a statutory corporation, Channel 4 would have to pay ITV £38 million.[26] The present prospect [1994] is that such payments will continue for the indefinite future.[27] Money that should be used for Channel 4 programming will flow to ITV without any commensurate return. It is reported that Channel 4 may now seek an amendment to the law.[28]

Under the Broadcasting Act 1990 Channel 4, from 1 January 1993, became a statutory corporation, licensed by the ITC, in the first place for ten years, but selling its own advertising time. In a final battle the government refused to succumb to pressure from the ITV companies that they be reimbursed for their alleged 'cumulative deficit' on Channel 4. David Shaw was reported as estimating that Channel 4 and S4C had cost ITV a total investment of £750 million up to the end of 1986/7. This, it was alleged, compared with advertising revenue of

Controversies in the Early History

£400 million. There was thus an accumulated deficit of £350 million.[29] The funding of Channel 4 had been the very reasonable price that the ITV companies had paid for their monopoly in television advertising, and the only excuse for the continuation thus far of a levy system which had left them laughing all the way to the bank. But whereas that victory had been won, Channel 4 was still to be the beneficiary, and the victim, of an unnecessary guarantee that was more likely to result in their feeding ITV than the other way round. But, I consoled myself, the major objective had been won. An independent Channel 4 and its Board could now fight for the survival of the cherished remit with its own money. In that essential point, I was satisfied.

NOTES

1. There are two books on the early history of C4; David Doherty, David E. Morrison and Michael Tracey, *Keeping Faith? Channel Four and its Audience* (London: John Libbey, 1988), and Jeremy Isaacs, *Storm over 4* (London: Weidenfeld and Nicolson, 1989).
2. Isaacs, *Storm over 4*, op.cit., p.24.
3. This paper was originally written before Brian Wenham's early death.
4. Doherty *et al.*, *Keeping Faith?*, op.cit., p.17.
5. Isaacs, op.cit., p.39.
6. Ibid, p.49.
7. Ibid, p.79.
8. Ibid, p.78.
9. See Central press release, 31 July 1984.
10. Isaacs, op.cit., p.139.
11. Alan Peacock (Chairman), *Report of the Committee on Financing the British Broadcasting Corporation*, Cmnd 9824, 1986.
12. See, for example, Colette Bowe's letter in *Campaign*, 5 June 1987.
13. His change of view was reported by Torin Douglas in *Marketing Week*, 5 December 1986.
14. From June 1986, Deputy Director-General.
15. See, for example, Phillip Whitehead in the *IPPA Bulletin* for October 1986.
16. Letter to Edmund Dell from Alan Peacock, 6 November 1986.
17. Letter of Edmund Dell to Lord Thomson, 14 August 1986.
18. In *Spectrum*, the quarterly magazine of the ITC, Summer 1993, David Glentoran, the Chief Executive of the ITC, wrote: 'Until the end of last year [1992] Channel 4 advertising was sold by the ITV companies and in many cases at a discount. Only now that Channel 4 is selling its own advertising time can the real market value of its airtime be established'.
19. Isaacs, op.cit., p.72.
20. He made this threat at the Royal Television Society seminar on 29 July 1986. It was quoted by Lord Annan in the House of Lords that December. See also *Sunday Times*, 23 November 1986.

The Making of Channel 4

21. 'We will not stand idly by. We will be in there fighting for revenues and viewers. We will do everything we can to be better and to make sure as much money as possible comes to us', David Shaw quoted in *Media World*, October 1986.
22. Budd, para.119.
23. Alex Mair, managing director of Grampian, 1 Dec. 1986.
24. Paul Bonner to Edmund Dell, 14 Nov. 1986.
25. My final meeting of the C4 Board on 23 June 1987 resulted in the following minute which may be regarded as a splendid example of *de mortuis nil nisi bunkum*:

   > Jeremy Isaacs reported on the hugely important and indispensable role which Edmund Dell had played in the success of the Channel since he became Chairman of the panel of consultants in 1980. He had defended its independence, insisted on correctness in its procedures, urged the need for quality in its programmes and, in all this, helped it on the course it is on today. Occasional disagreements were outweighed by steady progress and advance. The Board unanimously expressed their deep appreciation and gratitude for his services as Chairman of Channel 4 and his role in the development of British television. Sir Richard Attenborough noted his deep admiration and affection, and profound gratitude for the integrity which Edmund Dell had brought to the Channel as Chairman.

26. In addition to the 50 per cent that goes to C3 via the ITC, 25 per cent goes to a Reserve Fund established by C4. The remaining 25 per cent can be used by C4 for current expenditure but, if not so used, is carried to the Reserve Fund. The Reserve Fund can only be used for the purposes of C4.
27. This is in addition to the longstanding requirement, repeated under the C4 licence from the ITC, that C4 should provide S4C with programmes free of charge; and to a further requirement that C4 should continue to provide the schools programming that, earlier, it had taken over from ITV on a commitment limited to five years.
28. The arrangement is now being phased out.
29. *The Independent, Financial Times*, 13 July 1987.

APPENDIX I
LETTER FROM EDMUND DELL TO LORD BUXTON ABOUT CHANNEL 4 NEWS

7 October 1983
The Lord Buxton MC DL
Chairman, ITN,
ITN House,
48, Wells St., London, W1P 4DE.

Since I wrote to you following the June Channel Four Board we have had a number of meetings together with David Nicholas and Jeremy Isaacs, and we have exchanged a number of letters culminating with that of Jeremy to David dated 23rd September and yours to me dated 29th September. All this led to the meeting on Friday afternoon, 30th September, when the four of us met again to decide how we should proceed.

At that meeting, I gave you my firm assurance that we at Channel Four wished the Channel Four News to succeed and that we would consider any request for help to that end. I hope that assurance satisfied any doubts that you or David may have had in that regard.

However I also pressed on you the belief of the Channel Four Board that we should jointly review the contract between us. Our object would have been to ensure that if at the end of a further year the programme was not meeting certain criteria of quality which are agreed between us, and a minimum audience of 750,000, we should then be in a position without further argument to terminate the contract.

It was your view, however, that it would be wrong to review the contract at this time. It would, you thought, be destructive of morale if Channel Four appeared to be distancing itself from the programme. Nor could you accept the audience target we suggested as a criterion for termination of the contract.

I replied that whether or not the contract was amended now, it would make no difference to the practical choices that would face Channel Four if in a year's time the programme was still not meeting the criteria we set before you. At that point it would not just be in the interests of Channel Four that the whole position should be considered afresh. It would also, I thought, be in the interests of ITN and of ITV as a whole. Moreover it was highly desirable that those responsible for producing the Channel Four News should understand now that that would be the position.

I therefore said that if you, for your part, were not prepared to agree to a review of the contract, I would be bound to write you a letter setting out the position as we see it and reserving to ourselves the right to act in whatever way we think fit if circumstances a year hence continue to demand it. You noted that you could expect to receive such a letter from me.

In accordance with that discussion, I now give you notice that if in a year's time, in September 1984, the Channel Four News has not satisfied the criteria which I repeat below and which, apart from the size of audience, you have not questioned, we will consider that the terms of the contract have still not been met in that the programme has not been produced 'to the general satisfaction of Channel Four'. In that event the options must include the prompt termination of the contract with immediate effect. We will obviously not take this step lightly, and it will certainly be a great defeat for both of us, but we would in that situation be compelled to act without further delay to protect the interests of Channel Four. I must also repeat for the sake of formality that a fundamental term of the contract has not been met in that the programme has not to date been produced to the general satisfaction of Channel Four and the terms of this letter must be treated as being without prejudice to our position.

Let me also repeat the criteria by which we will judge the programme. Channel Four has asked ITN to provide a programme of news and news analysis, and to extend the agenda of television news to include coverage of the subject matter listed in Jeremy Isaacs' letter of 23rd September to David Nicholas. We also want the programme to find and hold an increased audience averaging 750,000 viewers a night, though more if possible. However that audience must be achieved in ways consistent with the programme brief.

Looking now to the immediate future, we have received your recommendation of Stewart Purvis for appointment to the editorship of Channel Four News and we confirm our agreement to it. We wish him every success in that appointment. We look forward to receiving any proposals you wish to make to us for strengthening the editorial team under Purvis and, if necessary, for adding to the programme's resources. We shall consider any such proposals sympathetically within the limits of the funds available to us. We shall watch with interest how the programme develops and we are prepared to keep in touch at

The Making of Channel 4

various levels with those at ITN who are responsible for it. I suggest that Jeremy and David should discuss further how best this liaison can be achieved.

On a personal note, may I say how much I value the relationship which has been established between us. I am sure that you fully understand why I have felt it necessary to write this letter. We have to make plain our determination to act if, unhappily, your present efforts, together with any help we can give, do not succeed. But our great object is to see this programme, with its agreed characteristics, successful and I am encouraged by ITN's confidence that it can be made so.

APPENDIX II
EDMUND DELL'S PRESENTATION AT THE ROYAL TELEVISION SOCIETY SEMINAR ON THE PEACOCK COMMITTEE REPORT 29 JULY 1986

1. The Peacock Committee recommends:
Recommendation 14: Channel Four should be given the option of selling its own advertising time and would then no longer be funded by a subscription from ITV companies.

There are two associated comments in the Report:
 (a) if the option were exercised, Channel Four would no longer be a subsidiary of the IBA.
 (b) The Peacock Committee would still wish Channel 4 to offer complementary services.

2. The Channel 4 Board has considered the recommendation. We have decided, against considerable temptation, to treat it seriously.

What that means is that we will now undertake the serious examination of this recommendation which the Peacock Committee did not undertake before it made it.

3. First, however, a word about timing.

The Channel 4 recommendation would require legislation. That probably means that it could not be implemented for, say, four years. Presumably if this option were to be given to Channel 4, it would involve a major change in ITV contracts. Thus implementation of this recommendation is probably possible only if the ITV franchises are extended to permit of the necessary legislation. If the Home Secretary extends the franchises, he may be taking this recommendation (and others) seriously. If he does not, we can assume that he does not take it seriously.

5. Why do I say that the Peacock Committee did not consider this recommendation seriously?

First, because there is no evidence in the Report that they did. Secondly, because they never consulted us about it. Thirdly, because of their claim that our costs are now 'of a similar order' to the revenue from advertising. I do not know what that is intended to mean. It certainly gives a very wrong impression of the current relationship between the costs of Channel 4 and the advertising revenue currently invoiced on Channel 4 advertising time.

46

Controversies in the Early History

6. Moreover the following very relevant questions are nor discussed in the Report. I put them in ascending order of importance.
    (a) how would the Board of Channel 4 be appointed in the interim between the grant of such an option and its exercise. We know already what the IBA thinks about the idea of the Channel 4 Board having such an option?
    (b) How, in the interim, would Channel 4's relations with ITV be affected, and in particular their willingness to build advertising revenue on Channel 4?
    (c) what would the City think of a Channel 4 floated free of the IBA but restricted to complementary programming?
    (d) whether it is the implication of such an option that a Channel 4 Company would be franchised for a limited period as are the existing ITV companies and TV-AM? Would any such franchise be up for tender, a question one would have expected Peacock to consider?
    (e) how, if Channel 4 were to sell its own advertising time, and be floated free of the IBA, it could be restrained from all-out competition with ITV both in programming terms and in competition for advertising revenue, using the full potential of its national transmission system?
    (f) finally, and to the present Channel 4 Board most important, would it be possible if Channel 4 exercised such an option to maintain the complementary and distinctive service of which the Peacock Committee evidently approves?
    All this Peacock failed to consider.

7. Why, in the light of the Peacock Committee's failure to consider these matters, should the Channel 4 Board wish to do so?
    (a) We have been asked by the Home Secretary, all of us, to participate in a public debate on the Peacock Committee Report. In asking for that debate, he has not ruled out the option recommendation.
    (b) We in Channel 4 realise that, in funding terms, we are in an unusually favoured, even privileged, position. In a more competitive world that privileged position might not stand up. It is our duty to consider whether there is any viable alternative.

8. Our funding system has been one of the key factors in the success of Channel 4. But someone may notice that it is almost too good to be true. Someone, or some government, may say that this funding system could be justified in the first five or even ten years of Channel 4. But how can such a system be justified indefinitely? Is not Channel 4 just too insulated from the pressures with which everyone else has to live?

At least 13.6 per cent of NAR in the previous year comes in, currently over £135 million. Our commissions and purchases go out. Part, at least, of the cost falls on the public without their really knowing anything about it. There is the cost of a monopoly in TV advertising. And there is the cost to the Exchequer.

We are far more insulated from commercial and other pressures than is the BBC. There is no political controversy about our subscription. No Committees are set up by Government to review it. Our licence fee, what we call the subscription, is not limited to the RPI. If forecasts of advertising revenue are anything like right, we are virtually guaranteed a real terms increase in funding during the life of the present ITV contracts.

Do you wonder whether we do not sometimes ask ourselves whether it is too good to be true? On the other hand, viewed from another point of view, it would be a mistake for

The Making of Channel 4

Channel 4 to become the justification for the maintenance of the ITV advertising monopoly.

9. Then there are other associated questions:
   (a) ITV companies are saying that their monopoly is already being broken. Personally I doubt whether they yet have much to worry about. But if they had some competition to worry about, would they guarantee their continued support for the present funding system for Channel 4 in all circumstances? Channel 4 may now be the toast of all ITV Managing Directors. But it is not so long since ITV company chairmen were moaning about Channel 4, evidently oblivious of the advantages to them of a maintained TV advertising monopoly for which the Channel 4 subscription was the licence fee.
   (b) If ITV franchises are to be put up to tender, and I have no guarantee that they are not, will the present funding system survive? There could be difficulties. (c) If it can be proposed that, when the technology is available, the BBC should be funded by subscription, might it not at some convenient moment be proposed by someone that Channel 4 be funded by subscription? If that day is to come, I would rather see Channel 4 securer in the position of being funded by its own advertising revenue, and with some experience of doing it, at least if Channel 4's distinctive character can still be maintained.

It is in these circumstances that the Channel 4 Board has decided that it is not prepared, indeed cannot afford, just to assume without further study that the present Channel 4 funding system is eternal and nothing else will do. We have a duty to examine these matters even if others will not. The Peacock Report is the first sign that the Channel 4 funding system will be questioned. We have to examine how Channel 4 might be funded and yet retain its special character in a more competitive world.

10. There is another public interest question. Channel 4 benefits from BBC competition. Channel 4 needs high quality competition in programming. If the BBC with simply the RPI is going to fall in resources further and further behind ITV and Channel 4, then there is a legitimate question whether some competition in TV advertising, more limited than the BBC would have provided, would be beneficial to the system.

11. Among the subjects we will have to cover in our study are the following:
    (a) In contradistinction to the case of the BBC where the Peacock Committee was absolutely right to decide against advertising, might it be possible for Channel 4 to sell its own advertising without prejudice to its distinctive programming? After all, Channel 4, unlike the BBC, is already funded by advertising, i.e. it would not necessarily add to the total fund of advertising revenue required for television. Its requirement for revenue is far less than the BBC's would have been in the long run. Channel 4 would not be competing with ITV across the whole range of programming every hour of every day. So within a regulated system it may be possible for Channel 4 to sell its own advertising without prejudice to its distinctive character.
    (b) Then there is an urgent need to examine with the ITV companies and their sales directors why the advertising revenue invoiced on Channel 4 account still falls substantially as a share of advertising revenue below our share of the commercial audience. In this connection, interestingly enough, there has been no pressure

Controversies in the Early History

from ITV companies for us to raise our share of the commercial audiences to the original target of 10 per cent.

(c) We will have to study what safeguards there might be to protect Channel 4's complementary role in a more competitive environment.

(d) We will have to consider the implications for Channel 4 of the floating of Thames, TV-AM, and no doubt other companies. With benefits to executives employed by these companies including shares, share options, as well as high salary levels, will the BBC be the only source for the recruitment of Channel 4's own top executives if the IBA keeps its 100 per cent shareholding in the company?

All this is for the study we now propose to make.

Perhaps we will decide there really is no alternative to the present structure.

Perhaps we will decide that with some quite modest amendments to the present structure we can have the necessary guarantees and assurances as far ahead as we can see.

Perhaps we may decide we want the option.

But first we must do some harder thinking than the Peacock Committee permitted itself.

APPENDIX III
THE WHITE PAPER ON BROADCASTING THE FUTURE OF CHANNEL FOUR

Comments by the Rt Hon Edmund Dell, Chairman of the Channel Four Television Company, 1980-87, as sent to the Home Secretary and the Select Committee on Home Affairs. Published by the Select Committee.

The White Paper on Broadcasting confines speculation about the future of Channel Four by determining, first that the Channel 4 remit should be preserved and, secondly, that Channel 4 should have the responsibility for the sale of its own advertising time. The White Paper adds that, in addition to advertising revenue, Channel 4 should be able to raise funds through sponsorship and through charging subscription. Thus far the Government is unquestionably right, though I assume that any question of charging subscription is for the longer term.

The original basis on which Channel 4 was established was right at the time. But that was a different era. At the time ITV's funding of Channel 4 was a legitimate price demanded for the preservation of the ITV monopoly of television advertising. It should not be forgotten that the ITV companies originally wanted the fourth channel to be allocated to them as ITV2. ITV2 was to be their second channel in the competition with the BBC. ITV came to accept Channel 4, and the funding responsibilities laid on them, first because they actually earned money on Channel 4 despite its apparently uncommercial remit and, secondly, because they interpreted Channel 4's success as an argument for the continuation of the present ITV system. The argument ran: Channel 4 can only survive on the basis of our funding and we cannot continue to fund Channel 4 unless we ourselves are protected from too lively a commercial environment.

The White Paper's choice of the tender system for the allocation of franchises makes the continuation of the ITV/Channel 4 link inconceivable unless the Channel 4 remit is abandoned. But even if the Government had opted for the present franchising system, a combination of a much more competitive environment plus the changes in the levy

The Making of Channel 4

towards revenue rather than profits, would have made the Channel 4 funding link acceptable to ITV only if the remit was sacrificed and Channel 4 became ITV's second arm in the competitive battles to come. First they would turn Channel 4 into a public service ghetto, freeing themselves of public service obligations by transferring them to Channel 4 and making Channel 4 utterly dependent on their funding. If that proved not to be enough in the competitive battle, Channel 4 would be absorbed entire into the ITV system as ITV 2, thus fulfilling the original ambitions of the ITV companies.

The Channel 4 remit was never limited to minority programming but always embraced 'popular' programming as well. Channel 4's schedules have always contained a great deal of more popular programming. This was right for many reasons. The fact that Channel 4 has not been a public service ghetto has helped to win audiences by encouraging viewers to seek out what it is showing. Among the effects of this balanced programming remit has been to make it possible for Channel 4 to cover its costs and, indeed, more than cover its costs. Separation of Channel 4 from ITV gives the remit the prospect of survival and it is now necessary to construct a constitution for the new Channel 4 which maximises that prospect of survival without giving absolute guarantees.

Subject only to its two predetermined conditions, preservation of the remit and separate sale of advertising time, the White Paper leaves the future constitution of Channel 4 open to further discussion. Two of its illustrative options are a private sector company and a non-profit making body in the form of a subsidiary of the proposed Independent Television Commission. The White Paper argues that a private company would have greater incentives to efficiency but that the temptation to maximise profits might imperil the remit. The balance of these arguments is against a private company. The concept of an ITC subsidiary appears to be based on two considerations. The first is that the ITC will ensure that Channel 4 keeps to its remit. The second is that the ITC could draw on the proceeds of the competitive tender and the levy to make up any shortfall in Channel 4's income. But such a subsidy would, as the White Paper itself argues, diminish incentives to efficiency.

An Independent Trust

The right answer falls somewhere between these options. It is an independent trust.

One oddity of the present broadcasting structure is that S4C, serving minuscule audiences, is an independent authority but that Channel 4, serving the UK, is a subsidiary of the IBA. No need has ever been seen to place S4C under some broadcasting authority to ensure that it keeps to its remit. Given an appropriate Board, Channel 4 will stick to its remit without any need to share that responsibility with the ITC. Indeed it is difficult to see any role for the ITC in that regard, especially perhaps as the whole concept of the ITC is regulation with a lighter touch. This proposed duplication of responsibility can only be counter-productive. There is no reason to imagine that the Board of a future Channel 4 trust would be less determined as a defender of the remit than an ITC with many other, and different, responsibilities. The IBA was never required to ensure that Channel 4 kept to its remit. But the subsidiary status of Channel 4 resulted in much time wasting and some cost by placing over the Channel 4 Board another level of authority without the skills to exercise it to any sensible effect. The IBA's skills lie in regulation, not in the running of a programme company. Moreover there will be a continuing danger of a conflict of interest between the ITC's responsibilities for the commercial television industry and its responsibilities for Channel 4. There was experience of such conflict of interest in the IBA's

Controversies in the Early History

relations with Channel 4. Thus, for example, the quasi-responsibility of the IBA as parent of Channel 4 led to attempts to interfere in the evidence given by the Channel 4 Board to the Peacock Committee, interference which the Channel 4 Board found it necessary strenuously to resist.

Therefore the only reason for making a Channel 4 trust a subsidiary of the ITC is the possibility of back-up finance in the worst case scenario which the Government apparently fears. Here the Government has to decide whether it is in fact prepared to give Channel 4 absolute guarantees independent of its performance. It is understandable that Channel 4 should want such guarantees. Nevertheless while recognising the special problems created by Channel 4's remit in a more competitive era, it would be wrong to provide them.

There is a balance of considerations. Channel 4 should not be protected against all risk. But as a broadcaster governed by a public service remit, and yet seeking advertising revenue in an increasingly competitive commercial world, there is an argument for allowing Channel 4 to play off a handicap, in some respects permanently, in others time limited. Against this background, back-up finance is not necessarily the best option for the future of Channel 4 and if it is to be provided it should be through some such institution as an Arts Council of the Air, not from the ITC. But at least until it is seen whether this is really necessary, the better course would be to provide sufficient value in kind and in other ways in an attempt to obviate any need for further support.

I suggest a few examples. None of them would impair pressure on Channel 4 for efficiency.

(a) The cost of Channel 4's national transmission system could fall, as now, on the commercial television system generally.

(b) All commercial terrestrial channels should be required to promote Channel 4 schedules without charge on the same basis as at present but without any reciprocal obligation.

(c) Educational programming on Channel 4 should not mean schools programming. From 1993, Channel 4 should be relieved of schools programming so that it can use the time more profitably. By 1993, alternative technologies should be sufficiently widely available for schools programming.

(d) There should be no Channel 4 obligation to fund S4C. S4C already gets Channel 4 programmes free, and it is absurd that it might be expected in addition to make some payment towards S4C.

(e) The tax position of Channel 4 should be made clear in the legislation. It should be free of tax so that any surplus it makes can be put to reserve.

(f) The present programme stocks and other assets of the Channel 4 Company should be transferred to the new trust free and free of tax.

Revenue invoiced on Channel 4 now covers all directly attributable costs, even though its advertising time is still being sold at a discount. It would therefore be surprising if, with such additional help, an independent Channel 4 trust could not survive with its remit intact.

I would recommend that the Home Secretary should initiate discussions between C3 and Channel 4 on complementary scheduling. A continuation of complementary scheduling would be of assistance to Channel 4 in preserving its mandate. It may be thought that an agreement on complementary scheduling is inconceivable in an era in which Channel 4 is selling advertising in competition with C3. I do not believe that to be the case. The competitive power of Channel 4, if unleashed, would be very great. It has the advantage of a national transmission system and relatively low costs. It is of great interest to the ITV companies that Channel 4 should stay in its present place in the market. I believe, therefore, that such discussions would be of value and that, especially if encouraged by the Home Secretary, there would be a high prospect of success in agreeing a continuation of complementary scheduling.

One final point demands emphasis. Channel 4 needs urgently to prepare its future. It should have a rapid decision and freedom as soon as possible from the surveillance of its future competitors, the ITV companies, and from its present parent, the IBA.

Channel 4:
A View from Within

JOHN RANELAGH

The key people, to my mind, for the early part of Channel 4's story are, of course, the members of the board (especially Edmund Dell, Anthony Smith, William Brown, Brian Tesler and Glyn Tegai Hughes) and senior officers of the company and of the Independent Broadcasting Authority at the time, plus Lady Plowden and Lord Whitelaw. Hughes, who had been a Governor of the BBC, provided the Channel Board with regulatory experience. Anthony Smith has serious claims to be the 'father' of the channel, dating from his articles in favour of a fourth channel based upon a commissioning system and his membership of and contribution to the findings of the 1976 Annan Committee which recommended the creation of a fourth channel.

There are some people who were very important but not generally known to be. Ken Blyth at the IBA was the first Board Secretary (I succeeded him) and played a crucial part in the behind-the-scenes diplomacy that underpinned the channel. The first six people in the channel were Jeremy Isaacs, Paul Bonner, Joyce Jones, Susan Crowson, Ellis Griffiths and myself. Indeed, Paul Bonner was offered his post as Controller of Programmes, and accepted it, before Jeremy Isaacs was appointed, so Paul is probably technically the first member of staff. Susan Crowson was originally Ken Blyth's secretary, and represented an important element of continuity and connection with the IBA. Joyce Jones had been Jeremy Isaacs' assistant at Thames Television, and came to Channel 4 as his Girl Friday. Ellis Griffiths

---

John Ranelagh, Commissioning Editor, Channel 4, 1981–88 (Secretary to the Board 1981–83).

had been chief engineer at Thames. I had been with Jeremy at the BBC immediately before he took the job as chief executive at Channel 4. So the starters were very much Jeremy's people. We were there for a considerable period of time before others joined, and each of us was a jack-of-all-trades: I, for example, acted as special assistant to the chief executive, personnel officer, information officer, and commissioning editor for the first six months.

Justin Dukes and Frank McGettigan joined from the *Financial Times* in mid-1981 and played important roles in shaping the company during the 1980s. David Rose, Naomi Sargant, Liz Forgan, Andy Park, Paul Madden, and Carol Haslam were the first commissioning editors. The story is true that Jeremy first met Liz Forgan when she came to interview him for *The Guardian*, and at the end of the interview he offered her the job as senior commissioning editor for news and current affairs. Naomi Sargant had been Pro Vice Chancellor at the Open University for some years in the 1970s, and joined us from there. She was the wife of a great friend of Jeremy's, Andrew McIntosh, so, again, Jeremy's hand clearly showed. This caused problems: several board members considered that such appointments should have been made in consultation with the board.

At Jeremy Isaacs' instruction, I devised the commissioning system, and Colin Leventhal joined later and developed the administrative procedures governing commissioning. Larry Coyne was involved as a management consultant from mid-1981, as was David Scott – later the channel's company secretary – who was a consultant from Peat Marwick. Sophie Balhatchett, Peter Montagnon and Colin Callender were among the first independent producers to receive commissions. John Ellis with his colleague Simon Hartog proposed that the channel commission them to be responsible for video workshop and experimental commissions, thus generating the first internal debate about the nature of the channel. Victor Schonfeld provided the first legal/editorial conflict over *The Animals Film*, which I had responsibility for dealing with on behalf of the channel. Anne Harris developed the first programme contracts and policed editorial control.

Edmund Dell was a crucial figure. He channelled energies and insisted on coherence and consistency. He kept a disparate board together, a flamboyant chief executive under control, and a rightly inquisitive and opinionated IBA Chairman and Board at arm's length.

A View from Within

The important issues at the start of the channel, it seems to me, were:

- the political will that generated the channel;
- the relationship with the IBA;
- the commissioning process, and the editorial issues it involved;
- the relationship with the ITV companies.

After the channel went on air, central issues in addition were:

- the internal political complexion of the channel and its reflection in programming;
- the IBA's regulatory role;
- whether the channel was an active editorial leader, determining what it wanted and who should supply it, or a passive editorial receiver, responding to proposals.

On these matters, the IBA – Channel 4's owners at the working level, as opposed to the board – always struck me as being radicals in pinstripes. Colin Shaw and David Glencross were always encouraging initiatives and made plain that they would support new ideas wherever possible. Others might well have employed regulatory authority to secure a more commercial or restricted channel, and the pressures were great on both these scores. Their concern, as the channel developed on air, was about imbalance and legal requirements, not about new voices or opinions. They supported the idea that the channel could seek balance across the schedule, and not necessarily within each programme or series. On several occasions I had to manufacture programmes for balancing purposes: during the 1984 miners' strike; over *Greece, The Hidden War*; over a programme about Israel from a Palestinian perspective.

The IBA established a committee (I was Channel 4's representative on it) to review the rules governing sponsorship in an effort to secure an additional source of funding for the channel and ITV. I remember David Plowright of Granada resisting any change in the rules governing sponsorship, and Ken Blyth arguing strongly for a new, more flexible approach.

Jeremy came to argue that the IBA should exercise its authority retrospectively, not prescriptively, but this did not take account of the statutory requirements placed on the Authority, as was gently pointed out.

Still on the IBA's role, it should be remembered that nowhere in the various Broadcasting Acts was the word 'minority' used: that came from a statement of purpose written by Colin Shaw (I think it may have been the terms and conditions placed upon the Channel by the IBA). The Acts use the phrase 'to cater for tastes and interests not generally catered for by ITV', and this could have been interpreted in the way that Michael Grade was later to follow. In contrast, Channel 4 in the early 1980s would probably have argued that it should be against the grain and, for example, willing to show violence in programmes within the law (and even here might well have sought to test to see where the borders of the law were/are). The way in which some films in the mid-1980s were tattooed with, I think, an 'R', because they might be especially violent or sexy or coarse, illustrates this point. And, of course, the tattoo was soon seen as a great marketing ploy.

On the ITV side, Brian Tesler, from the board of LWT, argued strongly for programmes that would deliver ratings at the start, and Bill Brown, chairman of Scottish Television, was central to gaining ITV's acceptance of the channel, and its help. It would be difficult to demonstrate this satisfactorily, but with some exceptions (notably Bill Brown), ITV was very anti-Channel 4 and had grave reservations about Jeremy Isaacs too.

We knew our appeal would be minority and controversial, and in the weeks before we went on air I was used behind the scenes to alert Willie Whitelaw and Roy Hattersley. Whitelaw remarked that he preferred to see and hear minority views on television than in riots and violence on the street. Jeremy referred to me as his 'troubleshooter' (and 'figleaf' because I had worked at the Conservative Research Department and therefore gave the channel one of the stripes in its rainbow), and used me over a wide range. I acted as the secretary of the channel's internal committees, and for important meetings I sat in with him and took notes: this is why I knew so much. I was involved in the negotiations with Equity and the Musicians' Union who were worried that independent producers would be fly-by-nights and not pay fees and residuals. I was given the choice in 1983 of remaining in a management position as his special assistant, or simply being a commissioning editor. I chose the latter, but Jeremy still deployed me

A View from Within

from time to time in other respects. He asked me to work with him in 1987 on the channel's position on being separated from ITV, but since I felt we should stand alone, and he did not, nothing came of that.

At the first meeting with independent producers at the Royal Institution in 1981, Jeremy responded to a question about how much of the channel's output did he envisage coming from independents, saying 'about 15 per cent'. This, I think, shows how the strength and vitality of competition and market forces was a surprise to those inside the channel. At that time there were about 220 independent companies; this number had doubled within the next two years.

Party politics dominated the channel's internal discussions and policy. After the 1983 Conservative general election victory, Jeremy told a programme meeting that since the Labour party had failed to provide an effective opposition to Thatcherism, it was the channel's job to do so. This was a sentiment that a (later) commissioning editor, David Benedictus, voiced in the same forum in 1986.

At an early programme meeting it was accepted that one person in five is homosexual and that we should make programmes by, for and about homosexuals. This gave rise to the Graham Chapman series, *One in Five*. An early independent film from Brazil – *Brazil Cinema: Sex and the Generals* – that used pornography, it was argued, to make political points, was prevented by the IBA from being shown uncut because Jeremy refused to censor it. Another independent offering about Freud used similar techniques: only guerrilla activity within the channel prevented the programme being shown in its original state. The series *Greece, The Hidden War* caused a flurry, and was banned by the IBA from being shown again. Ditto with *Jesus: The Evidence* (for which I was responsible). *Diverse Reports* made programmes that, *inter alia*, argued for heroin use, ignoring decades of medical experience. Video workshops in Northern Ireland made ill-conceived propaganda for *Sinn Féin* in the *Eleventh Hour* strand: after one board meeting, Jeremy said to me that controversy about programmes emanating from video workshops 'will kill me'. It speaks admirably of him that to my knowledge he never attempted to control commissioning in this sector beyond what the law required.

I should say that I was very much a minority voice within the channel, so my memory and opinions cannot be taken as typical. I felt keenly at the time that the channel was trying to act along the lines of the majority report of the Annan Committee – as an 'open' broadcaster with little editorial mind of its own – and that it was irked by the clear editorial responsibilities placed upon it by the 1980 Act. An underlying element throughout the period was tension between those who considered that the channel should have a strong editorial line of its own (Edmund Dell), and those who thought that programme producers should have maximum freedom (Jeremy Isaacs). Indeed, Jeremy consciously appointed commissioning editors with little or no television experience so that they would not be equipped to interfere with producers once programmes were underway. Liz Forgan and Naomi Sargant, for example, had never been in television before, and between them they were responsible for at least a third of the schedule. Most of the commissioning editors seemed to be content with Jeremy's direction, and with the notion that there is no such thing as objectivity. 'Everything is relative' was frequently said during arguments about programme content. 'Relative to what?' was never answered. In my opinion, we recreated Mary Whitehouse.

David Glencross, then deputy director general of the IBA, attended a programme committee in early 1983 when the editorial slant of the channel was discussed. I was alone in arguing that the views the channel was giving voice to were coming from one corner, not several. Afterwards Jeremy came to see me and said, 'I do not want to fall out with you', making clear that he brooked disagreement only so far and, I would suggest, that he had as much a political as a programme agenda. I think the channel's output during his tenure confirms this. There was, for example, the *Union World* strand early on that was not matched by a business or owners' programming strand. How dated such preoccupations even then appeared. One might contrast the number of programmes we had on organised labour with the number on science, engineering or the surging Far East.

The channel had a marked influence on BBC2 in particular, and on the film industry. Jeremy's decision to pour substantial resources into *Film on Four* was of major cultural importance. His control of resources effectively determined balance and volume of expression, but I should say that he also actively sought programmes that expressed views he disagreed with. With a guaranteed income, a watertight Act, and monopoly buying power (and thus contracts of one's own choosing) over the entire independent sector, it is difficult to see how Jeremy and the channel could have failed.

Above all, the channel was Jeremy's. Channel 4 was a democracy

A View from Within

where one man had one vote, and that man was Isaacs. His intelligence, warmth, production skill and experience, and the respect accorded to him by programme-makers, made him the outstanding figure. He dominated every meeting he took part in and he dominated most of the people in the channel too. Very few were intellectually equipped to do battle with him although, if you were, he would respect and sometimes act on what you proposed. Some who, perhaps, felt put down or left out, referred to Jeremy with bitterness as 'The Big I'. I drafted the terms of reference for the two principal company committees, programme and management: Jeremy insisted that both be purely advisory to him. And, of course, as Jeremy in his autobiographical record of the channel, *Storm Over 4*, makes clear, he had severe disagreements with Edmund Dell about the direction and emphasis he gave to the channel.

This was a deeply serious disagreement that spread beyond personalities. At its core was a question: was the channel an opportunity lost or taken? Was it doing all that it could to break new ground, illuminate new issues, establish fact and reflect the country as it was changing so rapidly during the 1980s? Or was the channel resurrecting dated (1960s) concerns, catering to interest groups, accepting of simple opinion, content with chattering-class blessing, presenting polish as innovation?

Establishing the Regulatory Framework of Channel 4

SHIRLEY LITTLER

The Setting-up of Channel 4: 1977 to 1980

In March 1977 the Annan Committee recommended (Cmnd 6753) that:

- an Open Broadcasting Authority (OBA) should be established to take responsibility for the services of the fourth television channel. The members should be appointed by the government;

- the new channel should not be allowed to develop into another competitive channel or one which was predominantly ITV 2;

- the channel should encourage programmes which say something new in new ways. It should include educational programmes including those for the Open University; programmes made by individual ITV companies including ITN; and programmes from a variety of independent producers, some of them commissioned by the OBA;

- the channel should not be allocated until the nation's economy would permit the kind of service envisaged;

- finance for the service should be drawn from a variety of sources, including block advertising, various forms of sponsored programmes and grants from educational sources;

- the Authority should, unlike the BBC and IBA, operate more as a

---

Lady Littler, Assistant Under-Secretary of State, Home Office 1978–81. Director of Administration 1983–86, Deputy Director General 1986–89, Director General of the Independent Broadcasting Authority (IBA) 1990.

Establishing the Regulatory Framework

publisher of programme material provided by others than as a broadcasting authority; it should have the maximum freedom which Parliament was prepared to allow;

- the IBA should engineer and transmit the service;
- the Siberry Committee's proposals for a Welsh language television service in Wales should be implemented as soon as government could find the necessary finance;
- the OBA's programmes in Scotland, Wales and Northern Ireland should be adapted to the special needs and interests of the people living there.

The (Labour) government considered the report. There was support in the Home Office, which led in the preparation of the response, for the programme ideas put forward by the Annan Committee but there was considerable doubt whether they were financially viable without substantial government finance, which raised two other difficulties: first, the cost of a new channel in addition (possibly) to other claims for extra government expenditure on broadcasting; and secondly, the risks to the independence of the broadcasters and the traditional UK policy of distancing broadcasters from government. The Home Office therefore, *inter alia*, was looking for ways of involving the ITV system in providing finance for the channel. Just before January 1978 when I became Assistant Under-Secretary of State (AUSS) in the Home Office Broadcasting Department, Merlyn Rees, the Home Secretary, had submitted a draft White Paper on the Annan Report to the Cabinet. This draft was generally speaking regarded as too dull, cautious and orthodox, and the drafting of the response was remitted for consideration to a special ministerial committee chaired by the Prime Minister, James Callaghan.

The Labour government published its proposals in its White Paper on Broadcasting (Cmnd 7294) in July 1978. On the fourth channel, the government proposed that:

- there should be a programme service of the kind proposed by the Annan Committee, while pointing out that minority programmes could appeal to substantial minorities and did not need to be esoteric (in fact the positive programme requirements proposed were remarkably similar to those in the 1980 bill);
- the service would be a single service throughout the UK in the first

instance, except in Wales where an enlarged Welsh language service, of the kind proposed in Option 1 of the Littler working party report on the Welsh television fourth channel project, would have priority;

- the service would be expected to rely on the ITV companies, especially in the early years, for a significant part of its output and for a regular supply of programmes, though these would need to be of an appropriate character;

- the service would include programmes from a wide variety of sources, in particular from independent producers, and should develop a distinctive new character of its own;

- the service should be run by a new OBA appointed by government which would provide, but not itself make, the programmes for the service and exercise overall supervision of the channel in the public interest; in particular it would ensure, as did the other broadcasting authorities, that the service conformed to the same basic programme standards as regards impartiality, violence, etc (it should not however be required to observe a 'proper balance' in its programming);

- the IBA would engineer and transmit the service, the government lending it the money until the OBA could repay it for this;

- finance for setting up the service would come from government, which would also continue to finance special programmes such as Open University programmes; however the OBA would need to look increasingly to spot advertising revenues in addition to sponsorship and block advertising. The OBA would be empowered to make contracts for the sale of advertising time or to negotiate contracts under which, in return for a rental, its regular programme suppliers could sell advertising time during their programmes and get an understanding about how their programmes would be scheduled (a sort of mini-ITV arrangement);

- the OBA would need to consult the IBA about arrangements affecting the ITV system and the possibility of complementary scheduling, and would also need to consult government about the service as long as it was in receipt of government funding;

Establishing the Regulatory Framework

- the government proposals would be incorporated in a bill to be introduced as soon as possible.

Both the IBA and the ITV companies disliked the proposals and Home Office ministers and officials were (privately) doubtful whether they were financially viable, though we put a tough face on it, for instance in arguments with the ITV companies. I remember telling Ward Thomas (Trident Television) that the government would make it impossible for ITV not to co-operate if need be. In the event, very little further work was done on these proposals because it was accepted that no bill would be introduced before the General Election. The only action taken during the 1978–79 parliamentary session was to pass a bill enabling the IBA to continue the engineering work on the channel.

Following the election in May 1979, William Whitelaw became Home Secretary. The Queen's Speech announced that a bill would be introduced to extend the life of the IBA, which would be given responsibility, subject to strict safeguards, for the fourth television channel.

Given the timetable it was obviously not possible to publish proposals in the form of a White Paper. Work went on busily in the Home Office, with a view to securing the agreement of the Home Affairs Committee in July for the preparation of instructions to Parliamentary Counsel to prepare a bill. The intention was then that the Home Secretary would indicate the main shape of the proposals at the Royal Television Society (RTS) symposium in Cambridge in September 1979.

As I recall it, the two main problems in June–July 1979 were: who should sell the advertising for the fourth channel and Welsh language programmes. There was a very strong lobby in government, led by the Department of Industry and supported by the advertising industry, through ISBA and the IPA, for a popular programme service which should be directly competitive with ITV. The Home Secretary, who took the view that the interests of viewers should take precedence over the interests of advertisers, beat off this challenge. Although the *Conservative Manifesto for Wales* had promised a Welsh language fourth television service in Wales, and this had been confirmed by the Secretary of State for Wales on 23 May, there were strong doubts about whether such a service was viable. It was unlikely to attract significant advertising (especially as the BBC refused to allow its programmes to be interrupted by advertising). There was also concern that English language speakers in Wales should not be deprived of an interesting new programme service – this was always going to be a problem unless there was one more service in Wales than in the rest of the United Kingdom.

In his RTS speech, the Home Secretary said that he started from the proposition that the fourth channel should offer a distinctive service of its own. There would be programmes appealing to and stimulating tastes and interests not adequately provided for in the existing channels, though the proportions of the population concerned might in some cases be numbered in millions. The IBA would run it. Finance would come from the sale of spot advertising, but not from selling time competitively against ITV, which would lead inevitably towards single-minded concentration on maximising audiences, with adverse consequences for both of the commercial channels and before long for the BBC as well. It would be a new national programme service, except for Wales, with at first no regional opt-outs, and it would start when it could be transmitted to and received by a substantial population throughout the country (the hope was 1982). It was not to be dominated by the ITV network companies: there should be a substantial contribution from the regional ITV companies. Independent producers should supply the largest practicable proportion of programmes on the channel and receive a fair return for their products. The channel was to be independent of the ITV channel for its programmes and its scheduling, The IBA would be responsible for the content of programmes on the fourth channel service, in the same way as it was for its other services, and should provide them as a public service in accordance with statutory requirements laid down by Parliament and without government interference in the day-to-day conduct of its business.

This speech naturally disappointed the big ITV companies and I well remember John Freeman (London Weekend Television) asking me how deeply the Home Secretary was committed to entirely independent scheduling of the fourth channel and explaining the advantages of complementary scheduling (as in BBC 1 and 2) in maximising audiences for the independent system. I was non-committal, but interested in this professional advice.

There was also much discussion of the possibility of DBS services and a suggestion in the winding-up speech, also from John Freeman,

Establishing the Regulatory Framework

that the fourth channel service would be made obsolete by Direct Broadcasting by Satellite (DBS) before it started. When I reported this to the Home Secretary after the conference, he thought it was pie in the sky and that two services of the kind proposed would immensely strengthen independent broadcasting and that we should proceed as planned. Therefore, we did.

There were frequent consultations with the IBA about the bill. As I recall it, however, the proposal to set up an IBA subsidiary to run the fourth channel came from the Home Office lawyers when preparing the instructions for Parliamentary Counsel. They thought it had advantages, notably as there were recognised relationships between a parent and its subsidiary company in company law, the precise relationship need not be spelled out in the bill. This both simplified it and exposed less surface for parliamentary criticism. The relationship could be allowed to develop over time as the IBA thought fit – subject of course to the statutory obligations for the service being carried out.

In the Second Reading Debate on 18 February 1980, the Home Secretary summarised the three main reasons why the bill did not provide for an OBA (contrary to the Labour party amendment):

- the fourth channel should not constitute a direct or continuing charge on public funds; there would be a reduction in the levy in the first instance but in the long run (later Leon Brittan suggested this might be three years) the channel should be financially viable;

- the fourth channel should not inflict serious damage on the system as a whole, as would an authority directly appointed by and directly funded to a substantial degree and on a continuing basis by government;

- the fourth channel should extend the choice available to viewers, it should not have the effect of restricting choice by intensifying to an unacceptable level competition for ratings.

The Home Secretary explained that the service was to be provided by the IBA, which would establish a subsidiary for the purpose of obtaining programmes and planning schedules. The IBA could assign other functions to the subsidiary, as it thought appropriate, except for its regulatory functions where it would operate on a similar supervisory level as it did for the ITV service: similar programme standards would apply. The IBA would appoint the board of the company. There were various safeguards in the bill to prevent the ITV companies dominating the service, notably:

- the positive requirements for a suitable proportion of programme material calculated to appeal to tastes and interests not generally catered for on ITV and for a suitable proportion of material of an educational nature;
- the provisions that the authority should encourage innovation and experiment in the form and content of programmes, should give the service a distinctive character of its own and ensure that a substantial proportion should be supplied by people other than ITV programme contractors.

As regards the Welsh language, the service would be required to broadcast a suitable proportion of Welsh language programmes supplied by independent producers and ITV companies, all the Welsh language ITV programmes going over to it when transmission permitted. However the BBC would continue to broadcast its Welsh language services on BBC 2. The total amount of Welsh language programmes would be increased as proposed in the Littler report and there would be requirements for consultation between the IBA and the BBC about scheduling them in the best interests of Welsh and non-Welsh language speakers as a whole, with reference to all independent advisers in case of disputes.

The ITV companies would sell advertising on the fourth channel in return for paying a subscription to the IBA, income and expenditure of the fourth channel being treated as 'relevant' for ITV levy purposes. In his winding-up speech, Leon Brittan noted that advertising interests were very unhappy about the way in which the ITV contractors had sold advertising and welcomed an IBA initiative to set up an Advertising Liaison Committee, on which ISBA, IPA and ITV would be represented, to try to improve matters. (My recollection is that the Home Office had pressed for some such initiative).

Although there were various unsuccessful suggestions by the opposition to assimilate the proposals more closely to those of the Annan Committee (for example, to weaken the obligation as regards impartiality from impartiality in a particular programme or programme series to impartiality in the services as a whole, and to substitute specific quotas for references to 'substantial' or 'significant'

Establishing the Regulatory Framework

proportions), the bill received a generally favourable passage through Parliament, apart from the Welsh language proposals. Indeed, in the House of Lords, Lord Annan welcomed the proposals in the bill as better than those of his own committee: 'The new fourth channel is really the same loaf, only now it is done to a turn'!

The main changes in the bill were that:

- the description of the service was altered from the second ITV service to the fourth channel service;

- the government eventually agreed to set up a separate authority to run the fourth channel service in Wales (the Welsh Fourth Channel Authority [WFCA]), on which all Welsh language programmes would be gathered; the service would be financed out of the ITV companies' fourth channel subscriptions in return for the right to sell advertising, with a right of appeal to the Home Secretary if the IBA and the WFCA disagreed. (Separately, however, the government agreed to a reduction in the levy which was designed to compensate the ITV system for the extra cost of this decision).

I remained as AUSS until July 1981, but in the months after the bill became law I was more concerned with the Home Office report on satellite broadcasting, local radio and the renewal of the BBC licence than with Channel 4. Others will be speaking of the arrangements made by the IBA and the Channel 4 Shadow Board and management to plan the start of Channel 4, which I think were brilliant – as was the choice of the triumvirate – Jeremy Isaacs, Justin Dukes and Edmund Dell, each of whom brought different skills to the task. Finally I might mention here that the first chairman, Edmund Dell, reaffirmed in his valedictory chairman's statement in June 1987 that 'the basis on which [Channel 4] was established by Lord Whitelaw was the best on which a channel of that kind could have been started'.

1983–90: Some Views on Accountability

I joined the IBA as Director of Administration in May 1983. By that stage constitutional relationships between the IBA and the Channel 4 Board, the structure of appointments to the Channel 4 Board, the level of the annual subscription and the pattern of meetings had been set. The IBA had also decided that Channel 4 would start broadcasting in

The Making of Channel 4

1982, and had postponed TV-AM's start until 1983, a decision which incidentally had nearly disastrous effects on TV-AM.

In practice in the years between 1983 and 1986 the IBA was occupied with a multitude of problems and opportunities: the various possibilities of DBS services; the re-advertisement of existing ILR services, the expansion of ILR and the costs of its radio branch; the IPA–Equity dispute; the difficulties of TV-AM; questions affecting the ownership of ITV companies; the expansion of the transmission system; and supervising a massive increase in the hours of broadcasting. From 1986 onwards the government had various plans for re-organising independent broadcasting more or less continuously on the boil. The IBA saw the development of Channel 4 – in which it took a great deal of affectionate parental pride – as only one element in a wider and growing system.

I was not myself directly concerned with the various disputes over impartiality in programmes. I was interested however in the constitutional relationship between the IBA and Channel 4. I noted that, in practice, Channel 4 had a great deal of independence from the start and took more to itself during the 1980s. In retrospect, I think there were three main reasons for this. First, the IBA spent far less time thinking about its relationship with Channel 4 than *vice versa*. In addition to the normal regulatory contacts, formally there was an annual meeting between representatives of the Channel 4 Board and the members of the Authority to discuss and justify the annual subscription, and there were meetings at two to three monthly intervals between the two chairmen, chief executives and senior staff to discuss outstanding matters, including programmes, money and appointments. However the arrangements for the subscription became set and the second group of meetings became less frequent and less meaningful as time went on. Over the 1980s, in practice the IBA allowed Channel 4 greater and greater freedom to suggest appointments to the board (including more of its own senior staff), to make its own senior staff appointments, to decide their pay, and to take its own line in public. Some of this was undoubtedly sensible, but decisions should have been taken positively and not by default. Secondly, the ITV Managing Directors and ex-IBA and IBA members of the board of Channel 4 felt inhibited about representing ITV or IBA interests there, which left the initiative with the chairman, management and 'independent' representatives on the board.

Establishing the Regulatory Framework

Thirdly, the personal relationship between the two chairmen, Lord Thomson and Edmund Dell, was not easy. As the channel prospered, Dell increasingly saw its interest as lying with the independent production sector and against ITV. He was seeking new outlets for independent producers from 1985 onwards and obviously thought that both ITV and the IBA itself needed a shake-up. By contrast, the IBA thought that the Whitelaw package was producing good broadcasting, which was the major objective, and it saw complementarity between the channels as being in the best interests of viewers. This meant give and take between ITV and Channel 4. The IBA was concerned to ensure that the subscription for Channel 4 was adequate – it was in fact generous because of the buoyancy of ITV revenue – and tried to be even-handed between Channel 4 and ITV on regulatory matters and programme issues, for example scheduling and the allocation of programmes in a two-channel system. However it never formally updated its view of the constitutional relationship between itself and Channel 4 to reflect changing realities. On my experience – and I said this at the time within the organisation – the IBA in the mid-1980s was not good at setting out clear objectives, or establishing systems within which its contractors were free to make their own decisions. There seemed to be an assumption that a broadcasting authority needed to be free to intervene in detailed decisions.

All this plus a very good programme service gave the Channel 4 chief executive, chairman and senior management increasing independence, power and prestige, and highly enviable personal positions in the broadcasting world, of which they understandably made the most. They had a marvellous remit, adequate and secure finance, the esteem of their peers, a vocal constituency of independent producers, much political sympathy, no need to make a profit and little or no effective accountability to their shareholder.

Looking back again, I think there were four reasons why Channel 4 had so much political sympathy. First, all political parties could feel that they had contributed to the design of Channel 4 and that it had added a genuinely new dimension to British broadcasting. Second, Channel 4 had a powerful patron in Lord Whitelaw who could protect it against criticism from the right wing of the Conservative party. Third, the 50-minute long *Channel 4 News* at 7pm gave politicians much enlarged opportunities to appear on television. Finally, although Channel 4's staffing levels became less lean as the 1980s went on, the economy and efficiency of their commissioning process could be used as a stick with which to beat both ITV and the BBC.

Edmund Dell has spoken dismissively of the 'Shirley Littler initiative'. That initiative, which was put forward in 1985 as subject to negotiation, had two purposes. First, to try to improve the uneasy relationship between the IBA and Channel 4 by offering *two-way* consultation before making public position statements or issuing press notices – it was a genuine attempt to identify points of difference and to try to resolve them. Second, to bring up to date the constitutional documents issued in 1980, some parts of which were by the mid-1980s being honoured in the breach rather than the observance.

I thought it wrong – and still do – that there should not have been a clear, published and up-to-date statement about the constitutional relationship between the IBA and its subsidiary at all times. In fact a constructive initiative foundered because Edmund Dell preferred to distance himself from the IBA and the IBA backed away from confrontation: but the underlying problems of Channel 4's status and accountability, and its relationship with the IBA/ITC and ITV, continued until they were eventually resolved in the Broadcasting Bill debates in 1990.

In the period after Peacock, Channel 4 had a simple set of objectives to maintain the remit, secure adequate finance for it and keep as much independence of operation as possible. These objectives, if achieved, would secure the futures of its staff and its programme suppliers, as well as serving the interests of viewers. If this meant distancing Channel 4 from others in the independent broadcasting system, the IBA, ITV or ITN, so be it. With comparatively few exceptions, the broadcasting debate between 1986 and 1990 turned on how – not whether – the first two objectives (maintaining the remit with adequate finance) should be achieved.

By contrast the IBA/Shadow ITC had a multitude of objectives – to secure viable remits and futures in the new broadcasting regime to be set up by legislation for Channels 3, 4 and (possibly) 5, ITN, DBS Services Teletext, Independent Radio and the successor regulatory and engineering bodies. It was as anxious as Channel 4 itself to secure the remit with adequate finance and believed (as did the Channel 4 Board) that a safety net was needed against the more competitive conditions expected in the second half of the 1990s. However, it was also concerned about the accountability of Channel 4. It thought it right,

Establishing the Regulatory Framework

first, that the chairman, deputy chairman and a majority of members of the Channel 4 Board should be independent members appointed by an outside body and that the executive directors should be in a minority; and secondly that the relationship between the regulator and Channel 4 should be set out in a public document and should thus be transparent. These objectives were secured in the Broadcasting Act of 1990 which provided: that appointments of the independent members of the Channel 4 Board should be made by the ITC subject to the approval of the Home Secretary and that those members could be dismissed by the ITC if the need arose; and that the relationship between the ITC and Channel 4 should be set out in the licence.

The Impact of the Peacock Committee: 1985 to the Broadcasting Act 1990

The Peacock Committee was set up in March 1985 to assess the effects of the introduction of advertising or sponsorship on the BBC's home services, including the consequences, *inter alia*, on the range of quality of existing broadcasting services, and to consider the effects of any proposals for securing income from the consumer other than through the licence fee. The committee took evidence from a wide range of interested parties, including the IBA, and its radical conclusions were published in July 1986 (Cmnd 9824). As far as Channel 4 was concerned, it recommended that because Channel 4 expenditure was at a similar level to the revenue received from advertising, Channel 4 should be given the opportunity of selling its own advertising time and would then no longer be funded by a subscription from ITV companies. Channel 4 should continue to offer complementary services to those of ITV but would no longer be a subsidiary of the IBA (though the committee did not say what it should be).

The IBA was strongly against this recommendation. The Channel 4 Board Report for 1986–87 records that a substantial majority of the board did not wish to be granted any such option, but also records that the chairman (Edmund Dell) was in favour of such independence. After discussion, the board affirmed that it was content with the existing funding arrangements based on 17 per cent of national advertising revenue [NAR].[1] If, however, Parliament wished to alter the structure of broadcasting, the board would not wish to rule out in advance alternative structures for Channel 4 and would be prepared to discuss such changes on condition that any new changes ensured the maintenance of the existing remit.

In April 1988, the IBA published its own policy statement for independent television in the 1990s. As far as Channel 4 was concerned, the IBA stated that the remit and independence of the channel, both of which it regarded as important for the structure of the channel, were best secured by its present ownership arrangements. The interests of viewers should take precedence over those of advertisers, but the latter would be secured by some of the new channels taking advertising. The IBA believed that, if ITV revenue shares declined as these new services developed – a terrestrial Channel 5 and DBS – the new services might also contribute financially to Channel 4. In its statement the IBA said that the IBA itself had no desire to change the arrangements for the Welsh Channel 4 (S4C). It was expensive but could be afforded if the ITV system remained prosperous.

In the meantime the Home Affairs Select Committee took evidence on the future of broadcasting. Its recommendations were published in 1988. As far as Channel 4 was concerned, it recommended continuance of the remit, which had been a striking success.[2]

The government published its own proposals for independent broadcasting in a White Paper in November 1988. This said that the programming remits of Channel 4 (and S4C) must be maintained. The government believed that Channel 4's special role was best fulfilled by an independent organisation subject to the ITC's oversight but without direct financial or structural links to the Channel 3 licensees. Advertising should be sold separately: Channel 4 might wish to contract it out. As far as organisation of Channel 4 was concerned, the White Paper set out three options (described in the following paragraphs) for consultation, and the Home Affairs Select Committee took early evidence on these.

The Select Committee published its conclusions in March 1989. It noted what the government had said about the remit and about advertising and about the separate selling of advertising. It rejected Option 1 (privatisation) and Option 3 (association with Channel 5) in the White Paper – both of which were also rejected by Channel 4 and the IBA. It supported Option 2, a non-profit-making subsidiary of the new ITC funded by advertising, subscription and sponsorship with a minimum level of advertising guaranteed. This was set at 14 per cent

Establishing the Regulatory Framework

of NAR to be funded by the ITC with Channel 4 retaining any money above 14 per cent as a reserve against the deficits which were expected to occur in the latter part of the 1990s when competition from new services was expected to intensify.[3] The Select Committee also recommended that the constitutional, funding and operational arrangements between the ITC and Channel 4 should be published, that there should be co-operation between Channel 3 and Channel 4, and that the ITC should have a major role in ensuring that this should be achieved.

Simultaneously, the ITC in its response to the White Paper (March 1989) had welcomed the judgement that the programme remit for Channel 4 had been a striking success. It thought that the existing arrangement could have served Channel 4 well for a number of years, though there were doubts about the longer-term future. The ITC thought Options 1 and 3 unsatisfactory and favoured a modified version of Option 2, provided that the Act made satisfactory arrangements for the ITC itself. Thus, Channel 4 would become a non-profit-making subsidiary of the ITC, selling its advertising separately from ITV, but guaranteed a minimum level of income (equal to 14 per cent of terrestrial NAR) underwritten by the ITC. There should be arrangements for cross-channel promotion and complementary scheduling between Channels 3 and 4, and the constitutional, funding and operating arrangements between the ITC and Channel 4 should be set out, publicly, partly in legislation and partly in a document agreed between them. The ITC rejected the idea of a non-profit-making trust.

The ITC doubted whether finance for S4C could continue to be found from within the existing broadcasting system in the 1990s and proposed that there should be early discussions between the government, the IBA/ITC and the Welsh Fourth Channel Authority about appropriate arrangements for S4C after 1992.

The Broadcasting Act 1990 confirmed the programme remit for Channel 4 and established it as a statutory corporation responsible for selling its own advertising. Board members are appointed by the ITC with the approval of the Secretary of State, with *ex officio* membership for the chief executive and such other senior members as are nominated by the chairman and chief executive. *Ex officio* members are in the minority. Channel 3 companies paid a subscription if Channel 4's revenue fell to between 12 per cent and 14 per cent of

The Making of Channel 4

qualifying television revenue; if Channel 4's revenue exceeded 14 per cent, half of the excess was paid to the Channel 3 companies and a quarter put to reserve, and the remainder could be spent. The figure of 14 per cent could not be varied before 1997. Channels 3 and 4 were to publish details of each other's programmes. Channel 4 was to receive a licence from the ITC setting out the conditions of operation.

NOTES

1. Channel 4 received not less than 13.6 per cent of the previous year's NAR, the remainder going to the Welsh fourth channel.
2. I have been unable to check what it said on the organisation of the channel.
3. 14 per cent was regarded as equivalent to Channel 4's share – 13.6 per cent – of the fourth channel subscription plus the cost of transmission and regulation which Channel 4 would have to pay in future.

A Defence of the Independent Broadcasting Authority

LORD THOMSON OF MONIFIETH

I am sorry that commitments outside London make it impossible for me to attend the Witness Seminar on 8 June. I regret this all the more in view of Edmund Dell's comments on the relations between the IBA and Channel 4 during my period in the chair from 1981–88. I would have preferred to discuss these round the seminar table, but since I cannot do that I thought it might be helpful to set out my own views and those of the IBA Board.

I have neither files nor diaries relating to the period, but I have no reason to dissent from the details of the exchanges which Edmund gives. I agree with what Edmund says about the issue of 'due impartiality' in the early years of Channel 4. He fought robustly on this matter with Jeremy Isaacs, as indeed did the IBA. In any case due impartiality was, as he says, a legal requirement of the then Broadcasting Act, and in our view a proper one given the limited number of broadcast channels and their degree of influence. The IBA vigorously supported Channel 4's innovatory remit, while insisting on the duty of due impartiality. I also reminded Jeremy Isaacs that some of the most mould-breaking ideology in the 1980s was coming from radical right-wing think-tanks under-represented in Channel 4's output.

An early test case for the IBA was the film *Scum*, about borstal life. The IBA approved its transmission by Channel 4 and was then taken to court by Mrs Whitehouse. She won her case in the divisional court, where the IBA was strongly criticised. The IBA defended Channel 4's

---

Lord Thomson of Monifieth, Chairman, Independent Broadcasting Authority, 1981–88.

right to transmit this controversial, violent but serious study on appeal, right up to the House of Lords, and won. If this record of private pressure and public support is an example of 'regulatory recapture', so be it.

Edmund's views on 'regulatory recapture' reflect a fundamental difference of view to that of the IBA about the role of a regulatory authority in the special case of broadcasting. He contrasts the IBA unfavourably with Oftel, Ofgas, etc. But regulating the price of gas is a clear-cut case of economics, compared with regulating the quality of broadcasting, probably the single most significant cultural influence on our lives. Edmund's approach to the IBA's responsibilities seems to me to reflect the fact that his Cabinet experience was as a distinguished economic minister and Secretary of State for Trade with a primary concern about competitive economic efficiency. I repeat that an absolute arms-length relationship between regulator and regulated is more appropriate to the price of gas than to the quality and balance and diversity of broadcast programmes.

The IBA's general approach to broadcasting policy, developed over many years since the controversial introduction of advertising-funded television, was one of positive encouragement for good programme-making, rather than one of negative regulation. We believed that Britain had created a unique system of some value – a public service broadcasting system equal in quality to the BBC but wholly commercially funded. The special remit of Channel 4 with its ingenious funding formula was a striking extension of this philosophy.

The duopoly of BBC/independent broadcasting – in which the BBC had the monopoly of the licence revenue – certainly produced feather-bedded labour practices, but it resulted in a general standard of television that was widely admired in the world outside. The radical free-market approach of Mrs Thatcher's new government towards broadcasting threatened this system. The Peacock Committee was set up originally with the purpose of examining the proposal that the BBC should be funded by advertising, but went on to examine an auction system for ITV franchises. The board of the IBA sought to do what it could within the constraints of a public authority to win the battle of public opinion for the continuation of the tradition of public service broadcasting and, following a further Conservative election victory, to engage in an exercise of damage limitation.

The IBA's approach was shared by most of those engaged in

A Defence of the IBA

broadcasting. It was feared that Edmund Dell's personal views from his position as Chairman of Channel 4 would provide encouragement to those in Whitehall and Westminster who wanted to undermine the public-service character of commercial broadcasting and replace it with a highest-bid system which would be good for the Treasury and bad for the viewer.

Within this general consensus, independent television contained many conflicts of interest – between ITV companies themselves, between the companies and the advertisers and also Channel 4's splendid new breed of independent producers, between the IBA and the companies it regulated – including Channel 4, which it also owned. Edmund mentions that the early days of Channel 4 were fraught, that audiences were small and that the ITV members of the board were seriously worried. These were, indeed, the days when John Freeman, an influential leader in ITV complained to the IBA that the ITV companies were being 'bled dry' by Channel 4 with its self-indulgent exploitation of a guaranteed income from ITV. Edmund fails to mention how the IBA sturdily resisted this pressure and defended Channel 4 in which we believed strongly and of which we were very proud. The IBA was also the legal broadcaster. It had to approve programme schedules in advance and defend them after they were transmitted. The IBA tried to ensure as far as possible that these conflicts of interest resulted in constructive tensions rather than degenerating into distrust and confrontation. It saw its role as seeking to represent the interests of independent broadcasting as a whole in its competition with the BBC and also in its dialogue with government. It sought a degree of consensus in the way independent broadcasting as a whole faced the new developments in cable and satellite broadcasting.

We were inclined to feel that Edmund's efforts to persuade Channel 4's board to take a line more sympathetic to government policy was a breach of a collective responsibility which we felt Channel 4 owed to the IBA. This background may help to explain the tone of the exchanges with the IBA, the details of which are in Edmund's paper. It is clear from them that in Edmund's words 'there was no meeting of minds'. He declares his total lack of confidence in the IBA which under the 1980 Broadcasting Act had inescapable responsibilities of ownership and regulation of the channel which he chaired. He does not hide his deep hostility towards the ITV companies which had to provide 80 per cent of the independent television audience. And he was in a minority within the Channel 4 Board in supporting the thrust of government policy rather than that of the IBA and independent broadcasting as a whole.

It is also worth recalling that at that time Channel 4's ability to stand on its own feet and viably sell its own advertising was by no means as assured as it now appears with hindsight. During those years Channel 4's transmission was only being gradually extended. It covered only around 70 per cent of the country and did not include some of the more populous areas.

In the end the Thatcherite policy of the 1990 Broadcasting Act prevailed, modified and improved somewhat in its course through Parliament. Edmund's successors (and mine) skilfully lobbied to prevent the privatisation of Channel 4. Edmund has the satisfaction of seeing Channel 4 licensed but no longer owned by the IBA's successor, the ITC, and selling its own advertising in competition with ITV. But the price that has been paid is in the serious dilution of ITV's public service remit and a downward pressure on standards. Nor has the threat of privatisation of Channel 4 disappeared. So successful was Michael Grade in increasing Channel 4's audience share (while preserving its remit) and selling its advertising that under the arrangements designed to guarantee Channel 4's income it is now [1994] having to subsidise ITV. Meanwhile, the efforts to persuade the Conservative government to introduce legislation to correct this among the many anomalies of the 1990 Broadcasting Act involved the risk of that government returning to the idea of privatising a channel which had shown its financial potential to prospective bidders, letting the competition of the new global broadcasting marketplace prevail over the maintenance of public-service values.

WITNESS SEMINAR

The Origins of Channel 4

EDITED BY PETER CATTERALL

This witness seminar on the origins of Channel 4 was held at the Institute of Historical Research on 8 June 1994, and introduced by a paper by Dr Peter Catterall, Institute of Contemporary British History.

Chair: John Tusa, Managing Director, BBC World Service, 1986–92

The witnesses round the table were:

Lord Annan (Chairman, Committee on the Future of Broadcasting 1974–77)
Kenneth Blyth (Secretary to the Channel 4 Board, 1980–81)
Paul Bonner (Channel Controller, Channel 4, 1980–83, Executive Director and Programme Controller, Channel 4, 1983–87)
Edmund Dell (Chairman, Channel 4, 1980–87)
Justin Dukes (Managing Director, Channel 4, 1981–88)
Roger Graef (Director, Channel 4, 1980–85)
Jeremy Isaacs (Chief Executive, Channel 4, 1981–87)
Lady Littler (Assistant Under-Secretary of State, Home Office 1978–83)
Anthony Pragnell (Deputy Director-General, Independent Broadcasting Authority (IBA), 1961–83, Director, Channel 4, 1983–88)
Colin Shaw (Director of Television, IBA, 1977–83, Director, Programme Planning Secretariat, Independent Television Companies Association, 1983–87)
Anthony Smith (Director, Channel 4, 1980–84)
Brian Tesler (Managing Director (1976–90) and Chairman (1984–92), London Weekend Television, Director, ITN, 1979–90, Director, Channel 4, 1980–85)
Sir Brian Young (Director-General, IBA, 1970–82)

The Making of Channel 4

Introduction

The idea of a fourth channel had been broached as early as the Pilkington report in the early 1960s.[1] Particular impetus was given subsequently by Anthony Smith's article in *The Guardian* in 1972.[2] However it was not until the Annan Committee report in 1977 that this idea began to take on the characteristics of a concrete proposal.[3] The committee recommended an Open Broadcasting Authority (OBA) appointed by the government which would offer new types of programmes and would be different from existing broadcasters in other ways as well – notably in being a publisher rather than a producer of material, taking its programmes from the ITV companies, independent producers and the Open University (OU). It also envisaged a Welsh language service in Wales, when finance permitted. This proposal was strongly supported by MPs, notably Phillip Whitehead.[4] However, little progress was made until the Labour government fell in May 1979 beyond a White Paper in July 1978,[5] the arrangements of which were disliked by the IBA and the ITV companies, and were privately considered by Home Office officials to be financially unviable.

These issues of the relationship of the new channel with the IBA and the ITV companies were running themes throughout the period under review at this seminar. As the incoming Home Secretary, Lord Whitelaw, came to grapple with the issue there was considerable pressure from the Department of Industry and advertisers for it to be a popular channel, selling slots in competition to ITV. Whitelaw made clear, in his 1979 Royal Television Society speech, his adherence to the vision of a distinctive service offering programmes to tastes and interests not adequately served on the existing channels, and he took the view that the IBA should run it. This view appears to be based on the advice of Home Office lawyers.

The subsequent Broadcasting Act of 1980 which established the new Channel also covered its relationship with the ITV companies. They were to sell advertising on the fourth channel in return for a subscription to the IBA, but they were not to dominate programming, though they would be represented on the Channel 4 Board. This Board originated with a panel of consultants set up while the bill was in passage. In December 1980 the panel became the Board. At the same time, its remit was agreed in terms of reference written with the IBA

Witness Seminar

and its own Programme Policy Statement (PPS), largely inspired by Tony Smith, with its commitment to innovatory television and to catering for, as the legislation put it, 'tastes and interests not generally catered for' on the existing commercial channel. This ambitious objective was soon to be put to the test. In less than two years, on 2 November 1982, Channel 4 came on the air. Before the new Channel appeared Brian Wenham, then controller at BBC2, had said that he would be surprised if the new channel achieved an initial audience share of over 12 per cent or under 4 per cent.[6] Jeremy Isaacs, who had been appointed Chief Executive in September 1980, had talked of 10 per cent as an initial target. In the event after an initial 6 per cent share, this fell to 3 per cent in February 1983, a performance that was not helped by the Independent Producers Association/Equity dispute. Meanwhile, the new Channel was attacked in the press, particularly by the *Daily Mail*.

As with all channels, Channel 4 had an obligation to due impartiality to balance its output. In the event too many programmes, it was widely felt, had a left-wing bias. Edmund Dell, the Chairman, was also concerned that the Channel's commitment to giving space to minority voices was being over-emphasised in relationship to its editorial responsibility to ensure that these programmes were well made and actually watchable. Edmund in a paper distributed to all the participants before this seminar has drawn particular attention to *The Friday Alternative*, International Broadcasting Trust (IBT), *Questions of Leadership*, *Channel 4 News* and *Greece: The Hidden War*. However, other early programmes such as *The Animals Film* could also be highlighted.

The appearance of TV-AM in 1983 was beneficial for Channel 4, as the press now had something else to condemn. By the Channel's second anniversary in 1984 it seemed to have achieved a remarkable turnaround in the public esteem, and even in the *Daily Mail*; Mary Kenny wrote there in 1984, 'to be sure, it still caters for minority tastes, and so it should, but it does not matter if the interest is a minority one, so long as the programme is well done.'[7] This is not to say that there were not continuing problems, as the New Year's Eve live broadcast in 1986 or the Greek civil war series that year demonstrated. It might be debated meanwhile how much the improvement in esteem for Channel 4, and its audience figures, reflected soaps such as *Brookside* and American imports rather than the fulfilment of the PPS. This certainly did not meet the Chairman's hopes of a more upmarket product, but how far did it meet other figures' hopes and expectations?

At the same time, the issue of relations with the IBA and ITV companies had not gone away. There were conflicts over the quality of *Channel 4 News*, produced by ITN, and over the amount of material produced by independent producers on Channel 4, as opposed to the ITV companies. The new Channel enormously stimulated the growth of these independent producers but it has been suggested that their share of scheduling was not always welcomed by ITV companies. Shirley Littler's attempt in 1985 to review the relationship between the IBA and an increasingly independent-minded and self-confident Channel 4 also occasioned friction. Nor had the matter of financial arrangements gone away. The levy on the ITV companies had been reduced in the 1980 Act to compensate them for their subscription to Channel 4. By 1983, Mrs Thatcher was concerned that this was having a detrimental effect on Treasury revenues, nor was it having as much effect as desired on improving the efficiency of the ITV companies.[8] The subsequent Peacock inquiry set up in 1985 pointed out that the advertising revenue increases did not seem to be matched by increases in the levy, which was based on profits. The Peacock Report in 1986 also recommended that as revenue for advertising on Channel 4 was now at a similar level to expenditure, Channel 4 should be able to sell its own advertising.[9] However the IBA was opposed. Their view was justified in part by the likely impact on advertising revenue for other areas of IBA activity. Meanwhile, the voices raised in support of this idea on the Channel 4 Board were effectively confined to Edmund Dell and Lord Blake. It was however an idea accepted by the government in its November 1988 White Paper.[10] By 1989 both the IBA and the Channel 4 Board had come round to variants on the government's proposals. The resulting Broadcasting Act of 1990 established Channel 4 as a statutory corporation responsible for selling its own advertising (from 1 January 1993). Under this the Board has appointed by the ITC with the approval of the Home Secretary, with some arrangements for complementarity between Channel 4 and Channel 3. Under the terms of the 1990 Act Channel 3 companies were liable to pay a subscription to Channel 4 if Channel 4 revenues fell below 14 per cent of qualifying TV revenue; if it exceeded 14 per cent, as it consistently did, half the excess was paid to Channel 3 companies, and a quarter held in reserve. The figure of 14 per cent could not be varied under the Act until 1997. [The prescribed minimum distribution to Channel 3 companies (once revenues exceeded the prescribed 14 per cent threshold) was reduced to 33.3 per cent in 1998. Culture Secretary, Chris Smith, has signalled his intention to reduce this minimum distribution to nil.]

This brief resumé of Channel 4 history raises a number of issues for discussion today. This discussion perhaps most naturally falls into four chronological phases; 1977–80, when we might consider the relative contributions of Channel 4's progenitors; 1980–82, the rush to be in a position to broadcast; 1982–86, the initial response and the building of a reputation and an audience; and 1986–90, Peacock and after. We might consider how these objectives have been interpreted and how far they have been achieved. There are a number of other things which run through these periods, both the evolving relationship of Channel 4 to the IBA and the ITV companies; related to this issue are the financial arrangements of Channel 4 and whether it should sell its own advertising or not. We might conclude this seminar by assessing the achievements and impacts of Channel 4. Tony Smith told the Broadcasting Research Unit enquiry in the late 1980s that the important objective was to shake up the BBC.[11] How far has Channel 4 achieved its own objectives, and how far has it contributed to changes, in particular to BBC2? Finally we might consider what impact has it had on film and on the independent sector?

Discussion

Tusa: Thank you Peter, an impressive collection of questions, and as he has suggested these four categories, let us at any rate try to keep to them. Shirley, you want to correct something straight away?

Littler: It was just the reference to Home Office lawyers, which is a slightly misleading one. The actual suggestion that Channel 4 should be a subsidiary of the IBA I believe came from Home Office lawyers, but of course, the suggestion that the Channel should be the responsibility of the IBA was Lord Whitelaw's, and I don't want the influence of lawyers to be exaggerated on this point.[12]

Dell: Peter said that Tony Smith inspired the PPS. The fact is that Tony Smith at the Board suggested that there should be a programme policy statement; the first draft was written by the IBA, I think it was written by Colin Shaw.

Blyth: I think the idea of the programme policy statement was around before the Board came to be formed. It was proposed as part of the relationship at a very early stage. Could I also say that one could trace the origins of Channel 4, and important influences on it, right from the start of ITV in 1954, when the intention was that there would be a second ITV channel.

Young: But a competitive one. I begin in 1970 because it was then that Peter Morley wrote a piece in *The Sunday Times* which caught my eye and it was then that Bob Fraser[13] agreed with his two deputy Director-Generals that the essential thing if the range was to be broadened, if the scheduling of programmes of high quality, not only high popularity, was to be possible, was that it was to be complementary. And so it was in the autumn of 1970 that we began discussions with the ITV companies, the assumption being that they would sell the air-time around the programmes, but there would be a very much wider range of providers, that all these things that we had talked about would be looked at – sometimes called minority programming, but there are better words for it. The trouble was the companies then talked too loudly and gave the impression in the winter of 1970–71 that the major companies were going to be in charge and that it was going to be more of the same, and this provoked a strong resistance.[14] I remember *The Guardian* particularly and understandably saying, 'Do you want double *Coronation Street*?'

So when we had a large conference in November 1971, to which I think Jeremy came, about what this new channel should look like, there was some resistance. In December we published a thing which in fact said all these things; we wanted to do a lot of things we couldn't now do and so on. We didn't get ITV2 (as we called it then) but we got an extension of air-time, which was something; but the BBC strongly resisted it in those days. The Ministry of Post and Telecommunications was very much pro-BBC and anything the BBC didn't want done tended not to get done. I think Sir John Eden[15] was planning to have a small group of three or four people who would look at this and I think the Channel might have got on the air seven or eight years before it did.

However, there was then the period of a Labour government, and

Witness Seminar

I don't share Tony's [Smith] admiration for the National Film Theatre or indeed the Open Broadcasting Authority [OBA] idea – they seem to me to add to our ITV2 idea only one thing, and that was an unsound basis of finance – grants from bodies, sponsorship and so on. They did however stress the independence if you like, and I think that must have been an influence in our saying in 1980 that what we wanted was a separate Board, because earlier we had fudged that a bit, we had talked about a separate programme committee chaired by the IBA. But a lot of people in the period 1971–73, before Tony was involved, were talking about the need for a fourth channel to do the sort of thing that BBC2 made possible for the BBC.

Well, there was then this hold-up, as I see it, where the OBA was talked about; but in the winter of 1978–79 Julian Critchley[16] (whose part in this has not been fully recognised) brought Willie Whitelaw round to the IBA, and the notion that it should be a complementary channel with the air-time sold by the companies, but very different in its programmes, was at that point accepted by Whitelaw. In May 1979, as soon as the Conservatives came in, he announced, as has been said, that it would be such a channel, a subordinate channel to the IBA. Then there were various negotiations that Shirley [Littler] will remember: he used a phrase 'with safeguards' – the IBA was to look after this new channel with safeguards; and she and we, the Home Office and the IBA, discussed in July 1979 what those safeguards should be. We were very much of the same frame of mind and it appeared in Willie Whitelaw's 1979 statement. In December 1979 we put out this thing about a Board and then got to work finding a Board, but I am now moving into your second phase, so I'll keep away from 1980–82; but I would say that the ideas that have been ascribed to Tony Smith were around for three or four years before the time that was mentioned, and people like Jeremy Isaacs, John Birt,[17] Peter Jay,[18] David Elstein,[19] various people sent in and published in this earlier period very much the main concept – the only difference was how it should be paid for.

Graef: I'll try and be precise. I represented on the Board the independent constituency, if there was such a thing. In that excellent paper you didn't mention – and I'm not sure how much one should attribute to it – the influence of the TV4 Campaign which did try, and was very much made up of programme makers trying to make sure that ITV2 in the form that we suspected it would happen, didn't. And hearing you [Young] now when I have the luxury of hindsight, I don't think we fully understood what it was you had in mind and we did believe that it was going to be simply more of what ITV1 had been, and just simply an excuse for a company to have another licence to print money.[20] So in a sense we were worried that this frequency would just be handed over, and not used for the kind of creative purposes that many of us wanted.

Also it is important to remember something which I don't think anybody is likely to connect, which was McKinseys' presence in the BBC in 1970, when they came in and having been paid quite a lot of money at the time of the Labour government their recommendations then had to be accepted because the money had been paid. They did not really understand broadcasting at all and simply said you have to set up these tremendous structures, the reference upwards – all these pyramids, because they used a form that apparently came from the Italian shoe industry I think; but it didn't seem to have much to do with broadcasting but imposed another layer of management on what was already a difficult situation inside the BBC.[21] So there was a feeling inside the BBC that many people could not do what they wanted to because the management was so restricting and so cautious. And although Granada certainly, where I then went, was a very creative place to be, there was a feeling led by the BBC that there were a lot of programme makers dying to get their hands on a kind of free space, so when the opportunity came in this form there were a lot of people ready to use it.

I'm leaping across time to go further to talk about things that some members of the Board would not know. Certainly Jeremy's statement in his MacTaggart lecture[22] that you saw only 15 per cent of Channel 4 air-time being available to independents was a shock; it was really very upsetting. I had been an independent since 1965, so that wasn't so much of a shock to me, but we knew that there was this tremendous number of film makers ready and willing to seize the opportunity and I think that it is quite important to understand that as far as the industry was concerned the perspective of both the Home Office and broadcasting executives was that they did not know many film makers. We started this short film makers' campaign back in 1960s; there were 700 members came out in Wardour Street, separate film makers in the middle of the 1960s who were making a living doing things that we didn't know about; we thought there were only 50 of us. There were

Witness Seminar

that many people who were waiting for this opportunity, and I do want to say, without going into enormous detail, that to me was what was most important to Channel 4, and I said this to Ken [Blyth] at the time, indeed to Whitelaw when he came and had lunch with me. I thought this umbrella, this way of funding, securing Channel 4 from having to sell its own air-time was simply brilliant. Having made films inside the government, having been on the Board of London Transport I had never seen anything like it. I thought that it was so imaginative, using the commercial tension that was there from ITV to support this creative energy that had been bubbling up really unrecognised. I thought what was really important about the first couple of years of the Channel was the fact that film makers were getting the access to do things that were unprecedented. Pina Bausch for four hours in the Sadlers Wells theatre remains to me hypnotic. I don't know if anyone in this room saw it, I still remember the images from it 12 years later; four hours of this hypnotic dance troupe with this kind of incomprehensible language was something no channel would ever have dreamt of doing, things of real bravery and that was saying that Channel 4 was not just different but structurally, conceptually, intellectually and creatively different, and willing to use its air-time and not sit thinking, 'Ah! we better reference out the Board, we'd better have a five-hour meeting to find out whether Pina Bausch is really OK.' It was the kind of atmosphere that was necessary for the BBC to be where it is now, to do the opera that it is doing now, to take the kind of risks that the BBC are taking can be taken back to Jeremy's willingness to take that kind of risk. As I say, I think the rest is history. It was a marvellous moment structurally, that the power was moved away from these pyramids that had been reinforced by McKinseys back in 1970, that existed in the ITV structures and allowed this curious linchpin through Jeremy.

One footnote to this and then I will stop. Justin [Dukes] and I had a disagreement about the amount of waste in the budget, Justin was very proud to announce the year-end results and say that we only have 2 per cent of wastage, and that shows how efficient we have been in commissioning. I said that I thought that was not commendable. I said that I thought we should waste more, and I still believe in creative waste, and the feeling that you could spread the money around and back talent and still not get it on the air is still important, still unrecognised.

The Making of Channel 4

Tusa: Is there anything specific from Edmund's paper about the early years of the Board and the period in the run-up that you want to comment on or contradict?

Graef: Well, it is not so much to contradict because I think his account is quite precise. The only thing that I would like to add is that I did feel that there was a structural gap between us and the commissioning editors. I too did not like the appointment of Liz Forgan[23] and David Rose.[24] I liked her very much, but I do not think that is the way to do business, and I was worried about this tendency to go off in one direction and leave us behind, so I encouraged two things. One was a series of dinners before the Board meeting where we could meet commissioning editors, and the other was that we would have the occasional weekend where we could talk about policy, which I thought was useful for us but I gather from the commissioning editors it was pure hell for them. It was an attempt to try and improve communications. I thought there was a problem there, we were made into ogres when we were in fact their supporters, and I wish that we had had a chance to talk about policy rather more.

Tusa: Did you find it useful or not useful that the commissioning editors knew so little about television?

Graef: Well, on one level I thought it was great. I think that some of us suggested this three-year limitation on their appointment and that no empire-building should happen, that failed almost immediately, after the first couple of people left. There is always this terrible cliché that everyone claims to know the language of television as though it were fixed, and the most important part about Channel 4 was that it changed that, and there were people in there that didn't know and their language was rather creative.

Tusa: Did it matter, as has been openly discussed by Edmund in his paper, that he himself knew so little about television and the people that made up the television industry?

Graef: Well, I think that it matters in two ways. I think that Edmund came at this with a different kind of expectation about the way that television decisions were taken, and indeed what television was. I think the fact that papers were worked over in Whitehall, and that things were done with a sort of care that ought to be found in television, and both Jeremy and I as film makers and Paul when he was a film maker did the same, it's not common...

Isaacs: I never did.

Graef: Well I did. But in a sense, because television is less important than we think it is, I think that Edmund almost exaggerated its importance. The IBT couldn't, I'm afraid, impose very much. I wish it had. I think that you [Dell] would have taken it a little less seriously if it could have done. So I think in a way you came at this as though every moment and every mistake in every programme was going to be embedded in history rather in the way that the details of your work were. *The Friday Alternative* was a complete mess. There is no question about that. I was just as critical as you were of it, but I thought that it was a good thing that it was on the air, I liked the trying. I am interested in creative failure and I don't think that it stays in history in that form. I think that usually it leads to something rather more effective. I wish that television were more serious, but on the whole it isn't.

Tusa: Brian, how well balanced a Board do you think it was in relation to what it had to do?

Tesler: I thought that it was an extraordinarily original Board with some remarkably diverse views, a rainbow coloured Board, that somehow worked extraordinarily well in spite of the fact that it seemed to have so many different interests, and perhaps contradictory interests represented around it. I think that one of the greatest difficulties stems from something that Roger [Graef] said, which represented a view that I know was very widely held in that first period earlier than 1977, from 1970 onwards. I was a programme maker at that time, not an executive, and Roger said that ITV wanted ITV2, wanted that fourth channel as another licence to print money. I think that that is not only desperately unfair, but actually wrong because what the ITV companies wanted was – and it is just as self-seeking but it isn't a licence to print money – the ITV companies had a great deal of unused studio capacity, a great army of under-used...

Isaacs: Over-paid personnel.

Tesler: Over-paid as well as under-used, yes of course, which was one of the problems, and a large number of programme makers who were offering all kinds of interesting programmes to their bosses which couldn't be used because they were not commercial. The ITV bosses, it had always seemed to me, first as a programme maker and then as an executive, wanted that second channel in order to use the capacity and the under-used personnel, and to give those awful nagging programme makers the opportunity to do those kinds of programmes that otherwise they could not possibly accommodate in ITV schedules as they existed then. Now the attitude that was expressed by Roger, and I think it was a rather cruel one – the licence to print money – was one of the problems about that first Board because that is what most of the others like Roger felt about the ITV representatives. The ITV representatives, Bill Brown,[25] David McCall[26] and I were being tested, it seemed to me, almost as much as the Channel was. The members of the Board simply felt that anything that we said was purely to promote ITV interests. I have to say that that was not the case: the three of us were obliged to protect Channel 4's interests within the rest of ITV, but for me that was one of the greatest tensions of the Board; otherwise it was a remarkably cohesive group of extraordinary unlikely colleagues.

Graef: What I said on the record here was an apology, if you like, for that view. I think, having listened to Brian, that we did misjudge the ITV position.

Tesler: Well, you misjudged the IBA position; you then attacked the ITV position

Graef: Sorry, I thought that what Brian Tesler was describing was the ITV position, but I just want to be precise about this. Brian Young offered me a place on the Board, and I turned it down originally because I thought it was going to be an ITV carve-up, and he said, 'I understand what you are saying but the people from ITV that we have chosen are so good that you will find that you can work with them very well.' And I said to him after the first year that he was right. I didn't feel that you were representing your own corner and if it came across that way then I apologise again formally and in public because I did feel that very well. What was a little more worrying, and I don't mind saying this to Jeremy in respect of that, was the feeling that Jeremy was an ITV person and had a kind of loyalty to ITV, and I was worried in the first year or two, with his 15 per cent limitation on independents, that there would be an old boys' network, if you like, that would be tougher for us to crack. That was not personal to you, but there was a feeling that there was a culture that we were up against.

Pragnell: I was going to make a somewhat dry historical point, but I think that it may somewhat tie in with what Brian Tesler has been saying; I wanted just to mention the pregnancy or the false pregnancy that began in 1954–55 because the authority has a duty to secure competition between independent television companies and it took that seriously, and the authority and the government of the mid-1960s was very near to getting a second service. In 1963 during debates of that year the Postmaster General said that if all went well, there would be authority to open a second ITV service of a competitive kind in three years, and it was only the arrival of the Labour government in 1964 which prevented that from happening. There were very strong arguments for a liberal policy in principle put forward by the authority rightly or wrongly at that time, and they saw what was intended by the initial Act which would be something more like the press – of a variety of people producing programmes. I suspect that all of us around here were quite glad that that didn't happen, but we did lose 16 years of this lid being put on the creativity, in the great frustrations that were put on people who wanted to do serious programmes being told there was no place for them and that the system had to earn its own living, so I think that one should just record that. Brian Young mentioned the great change that took place at the end of the 1960s which was the change of the concept of competitiveness to, I suppose, complementarity, because the Act foresaw that there was complementarity, making sure that there weren't the same types of programmes going out at the same time, and I think that one of the advantages of the 1970s was the move away from the sense of this mechanical idea of complementarity into this better idea of distinctiveness.

Annan: Just a footnote. There were lots of ideas floating around in the early 1970s. Tony Smith was the one who actually produced a plan, and inevitably when a committee is faced with a plan it looks at it. We didn't agree with the plan but Tony Smith is, I think, genuinely a progenitor of the Channel. Our committee was a rainbow coloured committee, though of course inevitably it was rather more to the green-orange-red side of the rainbow than the other. Again that was inevitable in view of the fact that a Labour government was in power. But our committee was much more balanced than a comparable committee would be under Margaret Thatcher. There was great suspicion among the members that Channel 4 was going to be another ITV2, simply more of the same, and we were determined that this should not happen. That is why we reported in the way that we did.

I think that the committee also had one other thing in mind which emerges in Edmund Dell's paper. We were keen to emphasise due impartiality. We did not mean that every single programme had to be balanced but that there should be a balance of programmes over a period of time. We had some bad luck. When Roy Jenkins set up the committee, he asked Edward Heath to propose a Conservative member for the committee, Heath nominated the man who had been the minister responsible for broadcasting in his government.[27] Jenkins refused to have him so Heath refused to play. Eventually we got two Conservative members on the committee. One was Sir Marcus Worsley[28] who was interested in local radio, and the other one was a formidable lady, Sara Morrison.[29] The trouble with Sara Morrison, who was an absolutely superb member of the committee, was that she did not see eye to eye with the new leader of her party, Margaret Thatcher. We therefore had poor liaison with the Conservative party at the crucial time when our proposals were being put forward to Cabinet. As a result [Conservative MP] Julian Critchley was the first person to rubbish the report as soon as it came out.

Littler: Can I come in if I might, because I worked in the Home Office on the 1980 Broadcasting Bill and it is quite interesting that the same themes kept coming up. The Labour government supported the programme remit and actually drafted the White Paper on this in very similar terms. There was a big question of course about finance and the extent of the involvement of ITV. The Labour government was quite clear that the ITV companies should not be allowed to dominate the Channel, but it was putting out some proposals for arrangements in which the sale of advertising might be contracted out to ITV companies as well as the Channel having its own separate sources of finance. There was an assumption that a new Open Broadcasting Authority would be appointed by the government to run the Channel. The big difference after the election – and this is why I think Lord Whitelaw must be one of the 'fathers' of the Channel, is that only he could have had the clout to see something through to implementation, I mean against the feelings of the advertising lobby that it should be a competitive advertising financed channel. He was able to say that you were not able to have that and keep the remit. He backed the remit, again with the proviso that the same standards as regards due impartiality etc. should apply as applied to other channels. He solved the problem of money in two ways because by making the ITV companies pay a subscription he made the ITV companies have an interest in its success, but also by saying that their costs were to be offset against levy. It wasn't direct government finance but there was some allowance against levy to help the Channel start up – but it was expected that the Channel would become self-supporting after a time.

The Channel was given to the IBA, which was of course making use of an existing resource (its transmission system). There were two other things which were extremely valuable in enabling things to grow and change. The fact that the Bill talked in terms of proportions of programmes sought from independent producers and others and not quotas, contrary to what the opposition wanted, allowed for change over time which was a very valuable flexibility. The other thing that allowed the possibility of change over time was making the Channel 4 company a subsidiary of the IBA. This meant that you could put general requirements about the safeguards in the Act but you could leave a lot of the detailed arrangements to be worked out between the IBA and the Channel as time went on. And there was known to be quite a lot of detail that could be relevant or not. Another difference between the Labour and Conservative proposals was Welsh language broadcasting...

Young: If I could just come in before the 1982 period, there are two things that I want to talk about: one is the Board. Edmund was wrong in thinking we wanted Richard Attenborough, because he was loved and respected by everyone in the industry. We wanted a chairman of Edmund's stamp, and we inquired of a great many people about a great many people, and a great report was given of Edmund, but he did not understand the ecology of broadcasting. It was thought that we were going to have four ITV managing directors on the Board and we said no we weren't; we had one or two admirable directors but we also, as a peace-making gesture because we felt that we had won the argument, invited two people, Tony Smith and Sara Morrison – eager champions of what I regard as the alternative solution – and it was extremely satisfactory that it did in fact sit together so well.[30]

Secondly, about the subscription. The companies said, 'We want to know how much is going to be taken from us,' and Channel 4 wanted to know how much they had got to spend, and I hit upon 17 per cent, which was shown as 13–17 per cent of revenue. We had a seven-year battle to make sure that a levy was taken not on revenue but on profit, which had some very good results as well as bad ones. I sent a draft to Jeremy before I sent it to the companies and he seemed reasonably happy with it. So that was the formula, 17 per cent of the revenue of the ITV companies should be the subscription and should be available to Channel 4. Those two things in the 1980–81 period were important.

Tusa: Thank you. Jeremy, would you like to take us up to the eve of launch?

Isaacs: Certainly from the time of Pilkington onwards one was aware that there was going to be pressure for a fourth channel, which was thought of for a very long time as ITV2 and was thought of as such by ITV and by ITV programmers, perhaps by some people outside also; and it was that expectation, a sort of natural justice required that in the end ITV facing the BBC should have two channels, as the BBC post-Pilkington did, that led ITV, with its surplus capacity in personnel and transmission capability, constantly to argue that the thing should happen, though of course they had their own ideas about how it should be run.

Secondly, there are the people who I think played an important part during the progress of the Bill before it became the Broadcasting Act, particularly through the committee stage, who wanted to make money out of being independent producers. They felt that they were denied the opportunity to sell their programmes to ITV and they were a very potent and quite skilfully organised lobby for the right to trade, to earn a living by making and selling television programmes in a domestic market in the UK, which previously there had no opportunity whatever to do. Thirdly, there were independents of a different sort – and those people in the end had to be listened to, and were willingly listened to. I remember a conversation that I had with a chap called Tony Morris who used to make nature films and I said, 'Oh come on, Tony, there are already so many furry beasties on telly, we certainly don't want another single one,' and he said, 'If you say that then you will be denying me and other people like me an opportunity to make some jolly good programmes that will also make us a living, so listen to us.'

And then there were independents who were of a different frame of mind altogether, mentioned already by Roger, people who felt that their voices were stifled and their skills unused, that they didn't have an outlet. They couldn't have an outlet on the BBC, because the BBC in those days only had programmes made by members of its own staff. They were affected by this notion that Roger described of the pyramid at the BBC. I vividly remember Norman Swallow[31] telling me that he'd left a job at the BBC because there were two people above between him and the channel controller and there were two people below between him and the programme maker whom he was supposed to inspire and commission, and an awful lot of able people felt stifled by this atmosphere.

I was made a governor of the British Film Institute [BFI] and asked to chair the BFI Production Board and came into contact with a lot of people who were capable of making interesting films, marvellous films, stimulating films, dreadful films, but films which had no chance of getting seen on any broadcasting channel then extant. They too had to be accommodated in the programming of the new channel which in the end quite rightly came to be called Channel 4, and not ITV2, as a result again of very effective lobbying during the debates of the committees of the House of Commons. I was quite wrong in Edinburgh [in the MacTaggart Memorial Lecture] when I assumed that because the set button said ITV2 it would be called ITV2; that was a very important change.

The job of making a channel would be to orchestrate the different output of these three sources. I was thought of, as Roger says, as an ITV person. I had of course worked for a long part of my life in ITV and I genuinely did think – though I was hugely grateful that there were no quotas specified in the Act whatever and no quotas specified in any document which the authority agreed with the Board of Channel 4 – that it was natural that programme makers within ITV companies should have an opportunity to contribute.

I think that the fathers of the Channel were Tony Smith, for the publishing idea, and Willie Whitelaw for banging various ideas together and coming up with an Act which became something that broadcasters around the world wondered at. I don't think that anybody else anywhere, and certainly not before that, had written a piece of legislation for broadcasting which gave so helpful a mixture of prescription and permissiveness to the broadcasters once they got in, and anybody who had a hand in that has some reason to take credit for it. I found it a huge help and security to know that there was an Act of Parliament that was trying, at least in broad and important ways, to say what we were trying to do.

Shaw: It was a time of extraordinary creativity, ideas fizzing around all over the place and it is very difficult, now looking back, to recapture really with any precision individual moments where things happened. I jotted down some moments, for instance, when the IBA discussed on 20 December 1979 the question of the title and whether things should be called Thames and Tyne Tees and so on. And I had notes of a lunch with Tony Smith on 16 August 1979 where we talked of a separate sales force with profits distributed to contributors to programmes – there were so many possibilities. I have no idea who actually had the idea that the trick was for the companies to sell the advertising and underpin the Channel in that way.

Isaacs: Willie Whitelaw.

Shaw: I suppose one thing that may be relevant, one of the last things that I did at the BBC before I left for the IBA, was to chair a committee which was preparing evidence for Lord Annan's committee, which was an act of self denial on the part of the BBC – to deny itself a demand for the fourth channel – and instead of that the committee thought it might stir the pot a bit and it put up a proposal really very much on Tony Smith lines. I had been influenced by Tony, and Michael Starks[32] had taken Tony Smith's lead and we put in his ideas, we were full of pretty metaphors about railway lines and who put the trucks on the lines, which was partly mischievous because we thought we would stir the pot, because we knew that the pot was being stirred in other places. But the one thing that people try to take away from us is the enormous sense of excitement, that I want to be nowhere else than in this place

Witness Seminar

at this particular time, because we were making something new and exciting for all the reasons that Jeremy said, and for all the reasons that Tony had foreshadowed.

Dell: Well, I've said a lot in my paper but at this stage, when we are talking about the very early days up until 1982, I really just want to make a very few points. First, I think that Whitelaw's idea for the funding of the Channel was splendid for starting it up. I did come to the idea, as my paper shows, that it could not continue for various reasons.

On the subject of the quality of the Board, well when I sat down with that Board on the first occasion I was in the position that there wasn't a single person whom I knew. It is unusual for a chairman to be in that position with a Board. But I think it worked well because it was a very good Board, and one of the things that I became increasingly aware of was the oddity that a body like the IBA, which I learnt not to have entire respect for as my paper shows, should be supervising the excellent collection of men and women who I had around me at that Board. The thing seemed to be the wrong way around. It seemed to me that the Channel 4 Board should be supervising the IBA. As to the managing directors, I mean I'm talking about the early years, I never thought that they were defending the interests of ITV. I thought that they were making a superb contribution to the work of Channel 4. Indeed, if you ask me what safeguards there were for the independents at Channel 4, I think that one of the safeguards was that we had such excellent managing directors from ITV on the Board from those early years. I think the rest of what I want to say will come post-1982.

Tusa: If I can bring in Anthony Smith, it will certainly interest me to hear why you think that your particular contribution had the effect that it did.

Smith: Robin Day had written a book some years earlier, which had actually introduced the idea of publishing on television.[33]

Tusa: Was that the critical idea, publishing?

Smith: Yes. It all started, I suppose, as a piece of historical good luck. I was on a committee of the Association of Broadcasting Staff [ABS] which was the broadcasting union as it was at that time. We were trying to find a way of stopping ITV2 from happening, which was being pressed for in the days when Christopher Chataway was Minister of Post and Telecommunications.[34] Some people were rather jumping the gun in ITV and were announcing that there was going to be an ITV2 or at least that there ought to be one; and then it was said that Chataway was about to make a statement to that effect. Some got together and persuaded him that this was not the moment. But then it became clear in the course of public discussion that there was no substitute scheme to fill the place of an ITV2, which at that point most people agreed would have been really reprehensible given the record at that point of ITV, which was not as culturally brave as it later became. It seemed to some members on that ABS committee that we ought to have a different scheme, a programme-based idea for a new kind of television system.

Tusa: A kind of spoiling operation?

Smith: No. In the aftermath of the failure of Chataway to announce ITV2 as had been predicted, we thought that someone should put together an idea for a new kind of channel that wouldn't be an ITV2 or BBC3 which in the context of that time seemed to be the only alternative. So we came up with the idea of a National Foundation, and the ABS Committee just about agreed to support it but all our friends in ITV, including Jeremy Isaacs, were opposed to it at that time. I wrote an article in 1972 in *The Guardian* and made a hundred copies and sent it to everyone I could think of.[35] There were lots of other meetings going on at the ACTT[36] and elsewhere, and Jeremy was also working on some sort of scheme. Then a year later *The Guardian* very kindly allowed me to rewrite the article taking into account all the things that had been said in the intervening year by other people, and then a little while later they let me re-write the article a third time. There were about eighteen months between each version and the article got longer and longer. In the end it was 6,000 words, and the editor Peter Preston said right, he would publish it, and Peter Fiddick (who really deserves all the credit), the broadcasting correspondent, said they would publish it a third time. The point of their operation was that it brought the discussion up to date in many different places, and gave us an instant tract because all you had to do was photocopy the article and send it round yet again. Then the two of them let me rewrite the piece a fourth time after the Annan report was published. I actually felt that I was just a kind of amanuensis for a shifting community of interested people. The plan evolved, but around the 'publishing' objective.

Tusa: Okay, let's move on. Jeremy, you were about to start as to how the Channel got on air.

Isaacs: I want to correct the notion that I in any way resented the idea that Edmund [Dell] put to me on the afternoon that he offered me the job of Chief Executive of Channel 4, that I had to work with Paul Bonner. I think I said that was an interesting and reasonable suggestion, I said I would ring up Paul and talk to Paul; we had a very jolly and amicable conversation, it was my birthday. We talked about a title – I wanted it understood that I wanted charge of the content of the output of the Channel and Paul accepted the title of channel controller, rather than programme controller, which left me in charge of programmes, which I was happy about, and I have to say that I loved working with Paul. I never for a moment resented his presence, it is quite wrong to say that I did, and without Paul we would probably have never got on the air, because I did not have then and still do not have the faintest idea of how a picture taken by a camera gets onto a viewer's screen. Paul understood all these matters and was able to bring these things about.

Anyway that was September 1980. My appointment I think began from January 1981. I was then finishing both a film with a Scottish murderer who later became a friend, Jimmy Boyle, and also a history of Ireland for the BBC at the time with John Ranelagh. And I would like to say in passing that it is not true what John Ranelagh says in a paper that some of you may have seen, that he wrote my application for the job.[37] Only John Ranelagh could have said that. He may have assisted me by putting it in the post or something, he may have delivered it, but I do remember Brian Young saying to me one day, 'Where is your application?' But again I do not think that there was anything set up or fixed about my candidacy at all, and I was amazed and delighted to be appointed. I had to listen to all sorts of rumours along the way, as to who was the more likely appointment. I remember Tony telling me at some God-awful BFI conference that we were attending in Nottingham that Paul Bonner was the man; one had heard rumours of Brian Wenham.[38] Edmund, I see, thought that John

Birt was the outstanding candidate, which says something about Edmund. How anybody who studied that 50 pages of application from John Birt, whom somebody (a member of the IBA staff whose name I shall not reveal today) very kindly showed me some years later, with its careful – I believe that John is very keen still on something called analytical data. This job application showed the different readerships of every single specialist magazine and newspaper in the United Kingdom, and no doubt offered guidance as to whether programmes for bird fanciers or for golfers or whatever would be the more successful. But the Board, apparently against the wishes of the Chairman of the Board, which I did not know then, and I'm not even sure that I knew it until I read it in Edmund's paper, decided to have me anyway. I'm jolly glad they did.

I am accused of appointing or seeking the appointment of Liz Forgan, David Rose and Naomi Sargant,[39] without the approval in advance of the Board, and it is true that I did act on my own initiative in those matters, because I heard ringing in my head the chimes of time's chariot telling me that unless we had senior commissioning editors in place as early as possible in 1981, and knowing that it could take three years for certain sorts of television programme to get made from a commission to an arrival on the screen – certainly two years, very often eighteen months or a year – I felt it absolutely essential to have good strong people in place as soon as I could get my hands on them, and I plead guilty to running roughshod over the Board's perfectly legitimate and proper desire to have been consulted in the matter. Yes, it is true that I wanted commissioning editors that did not come from television. Part of my feeling about the stuffiness and conventionality of a lot of British broadcasting was that we'd do better to get people from outside rather than from inside if we possibly could, so we put in this daft advertisement urging people who knew a good idea when they saw it and thought that they could turn it into reality to apply, and we deserved our fate, we got 6,000 applications. Paul Bonner and I claim to have read every single one of them, a vast number of them were from school teachers who were frustrated and miserable in their present work, and in the event we didn't take very many people from outside television at all. We did turn down a member of the present government who made the shortest of short-lists, Robert Key, later a Conservative Minister for Transport, who was then a teacher at Harrow, I think, and we cracked on.

Witness Seminar

There are two or three particular things that I should like to mention about the guidelines that the IBA offered to the Channel 4 Board or agreed with the Channel 4 Board before I arrived, perhaps as I arrived. First of all, education. The IBA, and Bridget Plowden[40] in particular, attached great importance to the educational work of the Channel. I think that 15 per cent of our output was supposed to be educational. By educational we meant work that was a coherent body of teachable material across a run of programmes. I tried to give education what it had never had in my experience of broadcasting: budgets as ample as other parts of the output.[41] In effect of course it never quite got vast and generous budgets, and therefore was accommodated at decent times of the schedule because it would have been insulting to push it away to other times when nobody could reasonably have watched it. That did play a large part in our schedule in the early years of the Channel. I must say that it probably hampered the growth of the Channel in terms of audience a little.[42] Nevertheless, it was an obligation which we undertook.

The IBA had originally expected us to broadcast 35 hours per week. Actually we got up to 50 hours immediately because I saw that we could with the aid of a great deal of acquired material, and I think that the IBA never really insisted that the educational output should necessarily expand to be 15 per cent of 50 or 60 hours or whatever it was that we got up to as we went along. That was helpful. The attitude that the authority took to foreign material was also terribly helpful. It seemed to me that when I arrived there was wonderful programme material, wonderful feature films of the sort that never got seen on British television, lying around waiting to be purchased, fairly inexpensive, that ought to be seen and that would attract audiences. If we had stuck rigidly to the notion of a quota of foreign material we would never have got that stuff on the air, but there were helpful ways around it. For example, if a film was a certain age, it could be represented as being part of the archive, called the golden oldies, but somehow they were exempt from quota regulations. If the film had any factual or informative or historical content, then that too meant that we could get away with it. This increased the range and diversity of what we were after, and diversity was something that I was terribly keen on.

Tusa: Before we drift too far away, I just want to tidy up the Paul

Bonner business. You have said what you have about Paul; I just want to hear for the record Paul's version of events if I may.

Bonner: I was the chairman of the Edinburgh Television Festival in 1979, and this buzz that people talk about, Colin [Shaw] in particular, was very much part of the committee that was running that festival, and we really did want to make some impact on the business of decisions about Channel 4. In fact what we wanted to do was to stir up a good debate, to try and influence thinking away from conventional solutions, and Jeremy was chosen by my committee to do the McTaggart Memorial Lecture job application. I became more and more admiring of Jeremy, but actually interested in the Channel, particularly in relation to the BBC which as Roger said was almost implacably against change. The Kensington House group,[43] of which I was a part, really couldn't see that you needed to get away from all McKinseys' empirical decision-making structures, and to recognise the two functions of broadcasting: one was that there had to be transmitters that had to be supplied with programmes to give the public what they wanted and sometimes what they didn't even hope to see, and there were people who wanted to make those programmes; and there was a real conjunction between the function of making and wanting to sell programmes, and having transmitters and an audience and wanting to buy – hence the commissioning editors idea.

Tusa: But you accept what he said about you personally?

Bonner: Yes, absolutely.

Tusa: Edmund, do you want to, in the light of what you said in your paper and in the light of what Jeremy and Paul have said, accept that you were mistaken in Jeremy's view of Paul?

Dell: There are certain matters even at this distance of time I thought not appropriate to put in the paper. I summarised my view in the paper but I in no way withdraw what I said.
Tusa: Well, historians have got three accounts to tease out, therefore, on the record. Jeremy, I would like to hear the impartiality/quality debate.

Isaacs: Okay, but first two things. When I said at Edinburgh that the

Witness Seminar

output of the Channel would be different but not very different, I was thinking particularly of the fact that we would be subject to the same regulatory body as ITV, and that we would operate under the same Broadcasting Act. That was already clear, and the person that kicked up a big fuss about it at Edinburgh was an admirable film maker and semiologist called Peter Wollen, a very distinguished fellow indeed. He represented in his abilities and his outlook those people who wanted to see a channel licensed to do all sorts of things which there was never any question that Parliament or the authority would bring into being. So I was simply accepting that in that debate in Edinburgh.

I want to say something about programme supply. It was helpful that the IBA did not fix quotas for programming that it expected from the ITV companies or from independent sources although later on, as comes out in Edmund's paper, it became clear that there were parameters which the IBA had at least expected the companies and the independents to operate within. It seems to me that between early 1981 and late 1982 and maybe even later than that, ITV simply went to sleep, they assumed that the independents would not be able to bump up the proportion of programmes they supplied to the Channel from the 15 per cent plucked out of the air by me, also revealing my ITV background and my scepticism about an independent sector. ITV got itself into a terrible tangle, trying to agree inside the 15-company system what the pricing arrangements would be for the programmes that they intended to supply to the Channel, and they could not agree. In that period, we were unable, even if we wanted to do so, to conclude deals with ITV companies whose programme makers and programme departments were dying to supply programmes to the Channel. We just could not get an answer from those guys as to what their terms would be; so much so that in the end we had to go to one or two companies that were so keen to supply programmes to Channel 4, and perfectly sensibly, not prepared to wait for federal agreement at Knighton House in Mortimer Street, and they agreed to supply us programmes on terms that we agreed with them before the rest of the network had got round to formalising arrangements. And I think that one of the companies that we did manage to do deals with in that time was London Weekend Television [LWT]. I had a broad predilection for letting every single ITV company, however awful its programmes, contribute to the Channel. We took a series of programmes from TSW, really probably one of the worst things that we ever put out, because I just thought that TSW should show us

The Making of Channel 4

what they could do in the West Country as it were. Into that vacuum the independent suppliers rushed and never looked back, and they altered the character and output and feel of the Channel because they were able to meet our need for programmes 18 months, two years before ITV companies could come on stream with their offerings.

Tesler: I think the simple and short answer is that the problem with the federal system is that it is a federal system, you have to get 15 companies to agree what the terms should be, some of those companies being very large ones, some being very small ones. It is very difficult to get the 15 companies to agree to anything. If it had anything to do with money you could imagine how very much more difficult that was. The result was that clearly the larger companies – with programme makers who had ideas that could not be used on ITV, that had studios with lots of space, who had technicians who were not used properly – were likely to come up first with packages of programming, and LWT was certainly one of them. Some of the ITV companies were better staffed with more organisationally minded programme makers than others, and the sort of criticism that Jeremy levels at John Birt were exactly the qualities that John revealed in his 50-page document and exactly the qualities that enabled LWT's programme makers to organise themselves to present a package of, we hoped, attractive programming to Channel 4 as speedily and effectively as it did so.

Isaacs: But the central point that Edmund makes, that George Thomson[44] quarrelled with us, and Edmund listened to these representations, was that we were taking too many programmes from the independents and not enough from ITV, and by the lights of those notional quotas we certainly were; and one of the reasons, not by any means the only reason, but one of the reasons is that the ITV companies were slow to offer programmes.

Tesler: I gave as a reason that most of them wanted to set up a pricing structure before they started offering the programmes to go with it. Some companies didn't and you identified one.

Dell: I'd like to make three points about matters that have been raised. One, John Birt. Now I know there are feuds within the television community which I am not equipped to understand; I apologise for

Witness Seminar

thinking that John Birt was a very good candidate. As to his 50-page submission, I am sorry that Jeremy did not read it at the time. I asked John Birt to give it to Jeremy when Jeremy was appointed. John Birt agreed. Apparently Jeremy didn't bother to read it. I think that is a pity; the Channel might have been better if he had.

Secondly, on the appointment of Liz Forgan. Now there was nothing in the speed and need to get on air that prohibited the Chief Executive speaking to the Chairman about that appointment. Now I made it perfectly clear to Jeremy that the thing about Channel 4 that most interested me was the quality of the current affairs output. Jeremy says that I wanted a Harvard professor or the editor of the *Financial Times*. I wanted somebody who would produce high quality current affairs output, and my gravest disappointment with the Channel is that we simply did not have that. Roger says that I attached too much importance to television and that if I attributed the right level of importance to television I would not be worried about things like IBT. For a person that did not get a television set until April 1979, I think that it is a little odd to a attribute to me a view of the importance of television, but what I did think was that Channel 4 had an exceptional opportunity, funded as it was to produce very high quality current affairs output. We needed a commissioning editor capable of doing that. We never had it. That was a source of friction between Jeremy and me but I was disappointed at the end of that particular relationship.

Tusa: Would you just like to add something, while you are on the question, about where your disappointment lay over the question of what you call due impartiality, and then Jeremy can answer.

Dell: Well, on due impartiality there is no doubt that in the first year or so of the Channel it had a left-wing bias. I thought that to be totally inappropriate and unnecessary, and I think it was damaging to the Channel.

Isaacs: I think Liz Forgan was an excellent commissioning editor, and I think that her subsequent career shows that my judgement was vindicated, and if nothing else she will be remembered as the person who bludgeoned and cajoled ITN into coming up in the end with an effective programme called *Channel 4 News* which is still one of the lasting creditable achievements of the Channel and long may it remain so. Incidentally, I and Liz did try and persuade David Nicholas at ITN that he should engage David Watt to edit *Channel 4 News*. It would have been very interesting if he had been appointed. As it was, ITN went outside television to find a reputable *Sunday Times* journalist to edit *Channel 4 News* and he turned out to be a hopeless editor. I just think that Edmund had a very lofty expectation of what we should be aiming at and that it was far more difficult to achieve practically than perhaps he understood.

That is not to say that I think that programmes like the IBT programmes were any good. They were programmes of the sort of lecture and discussion meeting that you have up and down the land in church halls of people trying to call attention to the needs of the third world. They were there as part of our educational output. I wanted the widest possible diversity and therefore doled out commissions and penny packets to see what people could do in the hope that the very difference of what they would come up with would give the Channel its distinctiveness.

I quarrel with Edmund about political impartiality, which did make life very difficult for me in those early years of the Channel. That doesn't actually derive from a categorical disagreement with him or with the IBA or with anybody else about the importance of political impartiality in the overall output of Channel 4; of course I knew that was a requirement and a requirement that I was happy to live with. I did, however, think that it would have to be interpreted differently on Channel 4 than it had been on ITV if the Channel was to appear more lively, more outspoken, more provocative, more stimulating than ITV or BBC had ever succeeded in being. Let us not forget that the BBC had invited E.P. Thompson to give the Dimbleby lecture. The invitation was vetoed by the Board of Governors of the BBC. I wrote to Thompson and invited him to give such a lecture on Channel 4, and steaming hot stuff it was too. Were we too left-wing in the early years? Probably we were a bit, I admitted as much at Edinburgh. It wasn't a deliberate intention to be so, it is just that there was a great flood of ideas and attitudes waiting, impatient at not getting on the air, and the ideas of the right that were then governing the country had not yet found popular proponents or protagonists of the sort that could turn those ideas into television journalism. Had such material been available earlier we would have made much more use of it. As it was we pandered to this notion that some people had that Channel 4 was going to be their channel on the left. When I, in this series of opinions to which E.P. Thompson had contributed, invited Paul Johnson to do so also, and he spoke very elegantly and beautifully of the market, viewers rang up to say 'What are you doing letting that man broadcast on our channel?' When we interviewed the South African Ambassador on *Channel 4 News*, people rang up and said 'This is a democracy, how dare you allow the South African Ambassador to appear on television?' and of course I was trying to confound their idiotic narrow repressed expectations of debate and diversity.

I don't think IBT was ever as important as Edmund made it out to be. I do know that it was a subject that was particularly important to him, and I know that we didn't handle it as well as he would have liked us to have done. I think that he is wrong in one respect about *The Friday Alternative*, which I am interested that Roger remembers with affection; it was never intended to be a left-wing programme, indeed steps were taken to ensure that it encompassed a range of political opinion. Not only was that a stated requirement in the commission to David Graham, an independent producer who later went on to distinguish himself by being extremely right-wing, but he was actually asked to attempt something which I gather is now becoming fashionable again called 'Citizen Juries'. I am very happy that we had a go with *The Friday Alternative* and rather sorry that it came to end so quickly.

Tusa: I would like to hear what outside observers like Lord Annan, Tony Smith and Colin Shaw thought about the perceived left-wing bias of Channel 4 in its early years.

Smith: The problem was that David Graham could not cope with his staff; he somehow found himself recruiting some very left-wing people without knowing what he was doing, and then he found himself being very repressive and stopping them putting on air what they wanted. One also has to look at film in general at that point; in cultural history, film and television had just come to be noticed by the left. Writers on the left in the neo-Marxist wave of that moment discovered television to which they had paid no attention previously. They had been concerned with the economic infrastructure, but the ideas of Althusser arrived from France and took over Marxist thought in this country. That happened during the late 1960s and 1970s and suddenly everyone was pre-occupied with the newly recognised cultural superstructure.

Marxists realised the ideological power of the superstructure, rather than the economic base. Everyone on the left was therefore excessively interested in television at that moment.

Tusa: But did the left capture Channel 4?

Smith: No,[45] but when it started there were a lot of people who were being influenced by left-wing ideas – very creatively in fact – in a variety of fields. Hence when Channel 4 caused IBT to come into existence,[46] by getting together a number of groups that wanted to produce third-world related programmes, automatically strands of left-wing economic thought came to the fore. The ideas were in the air, it wasn't Channel 4 conspiring to foster them. I believe any new channel starting up in Britain at that time would have met with the same ideas. If the film industry had offered more opportunities at that time, the same ideas would have found their way into narrative scripts.

Annan: I think that is a very good point that Tony has been making. I don't think that there was any doubt that there was a left-wing bias. That is because most people who want to make programmes want to make programmes against authority. It isn't necessarily party political at all, it is a genuine desire to challenge authority, to expose it and to be on the whole hostile to it, and I think this is the reason why broadcasters are accused of not being impartial. The only programme that I thought was a disgrace was the Greek programme, and that was because the people that were asked to take part in it were people who had been parachuted into Greece during the war; their statements were in fact falsified.

Isaacs: As Edmund points out in his paper, that programme was delivered by the stuffiest and most boring of the ITV companies, TVS, and it was my categorical understanding as someone who had made films about civil wars himself, that we would hear both sides of the argument in the civil war; we never did, and we didn't find out until it was too late that we weren't going to, and also that the Brits that had taken part in it had been deceived as to the content and the nature of the programme.

Shaw: My official connection with Channel 4 was only about eight months long when I was despatched from the stage and played no

Witness Seminar

further part. I think people are much more likely to be commenting on a tone of voice, rather than it being actually skewed in a particular direction. I never thought that it was particularly left-wing but I think we were concerned in those first eight months with trying to assure Lord Thomson that the whole thing was not going to go to pieces in his hands, because he felt somehow that Channel 4 ought to be getting a better press. The Board of Governors and Commissioners and so on do tend to get a bit twitchy when their charges don't do immediately what they think they should. I think he was distinctly rattled in those first few months.

Isaacs: John Whitney[47] asked me to take *Brookside* off the air after three weeks.

Bonner: It wasn't just the Marxist invasion of the media, but it was the stridency of the voices who felt themselves, rightly or wrongly, to have been disenfranchised by television. We built a mechanism before we ever got on the air to allow for some of this, called *Right to Reply*, but the problem was that it was once a week and really we would have needed to have a reply after every programme to achieve due impartiality on certain evenings, and what ultimately was done, as Jeremy has said, was a re-balancing of opinions. I don't think that there is anything historically wrong with that development, weaving one way initially, and then having to be brought back on course again. I don't think, with one or two exceptions, that there were too many programmes that lay outside the broadest parameters of public service broadcasting.

Isaacs: Anyway this was a tiny proportion of our output, that is why it was so tedious to have this at Board meetings. I don't want to be rude about it, but the fact is that it was not easy to get the Channel on the air. There were all sorts of balancing acts to perform. One had this vast amount of stuff chuntering out week after week. The audience was gradually growing and building and we were talking about IBT at Board meeting after Board meeting.

Shaw: If I can just jog back to what Jeremy was saying about education, I think that one thing that ought to be remembered was that Bridget Plowden and Brian Young played a large part in seeing off the Open University, which certainly in 1979 had very strong designs on taking part of Channel 4. I can remember going down to the Department of Education with Brian and Bridget and being talked to very sternly by the permanent secretary[48] who thought that Channel 4 ought to have a large slice of Open University time, and Bridget was saying that it was absolutely essential that any education time was given to those who had left school at 14 or 15 rather than those who were in a privileged position in tertiary education.

Tusa: Edmund.

Dell: First of all we did not discuss IBT at Board meeting after Board meeting. IBT, I thought, was a particular example where Channel 4 gave way to a pressure group. There were other examples. Actually, the first person to raise the question of the political bias of the Channel at the Board was Tony Smith, although it had been raised in other fora, and I think he was justified in doing so. I didn't raise it, although I was worried about it and I talked to Jeremy about it. I didn't raise it at the Board myself for obvious reasons, I didn't want to exacerbate what was already a difficult situation between Jeremy and myself. Now the idea that there were a lot of people with particular views around who had never had an opportunity to express them, therefore the Channel had to give them an unbalanced opportunity, so to do is in my innocent view absolute nonsense. The idea that other ideas were not around waiting to be expressed is again nonsense. They were around and they could have been encouraged. In fact the easy course was taken, and I don't know why Jeremy fights it so much. In the end he had to admit that this was a serious problem with the Channel and that something had to be done about it, and in the end it was. So it seems to me that it would be better if he accepted the fact that this was a mistake. It wasn't just a small part of our output, it was the essential nature of our current affairs output. It had a very serious effect on the public reputation of the Channel and it was a mistake. I indicated in my paper that it was a mistake, and I think that Jeremy should admit that that was a mistake.

Isaacs: I don't admit that it was a mistake to allow access to those people at all. I think that perhaps one would understand the situation better by looking more closely at the commissioning process; one of the mistakes that the Channel certainly did make was to underestimate the volume of submissions that we would receive, and the biggest single

Witness Seminar

difficulty that the Channel had in its first few months before it was on the air was coping with this flood of programme suggestions, because Justin and I had decided that the Channel had to be as lean as it possibly could be. I remember Paul and I agreeing that we would start with 48 people.

Bonner: We promised the Board.

Isaacs: Luckily Brian Tesler said, 'Don't be daft, you'll need 165.' The commissioning process was passive as well as active. It was a selection process; nobody commissioning – except perhaps David Rose at Film on Four – had enough time to stand back from the flood of people that were trying to get at him and go out to other people and say 'I want you to make me a film.'

Edmund is quite right to say that there was such a tinge in part of our output, and it was necessary to take steps to do something about it. I do think that its importance was exaggerated at the time, and I don't think that it was wrong to proceed in the way that we proceeded. When Willie Whitelaw took me to lunch at Bucks Club, he said, 'My dear boy, just be a little bit more careful will you,' and that was the right attitude to take, not the meal that we made of it.

Tusa: Those were the days, I am aware that it is passing…gentleman knew how to do things in those days. Shirley, do you have anything to add to this specific question?

Littler: Yes, just very quickly. The IBA, generally speaking, supported Edmund in his view of impartiality and what the programme obligations were. You have also made some unkind remarks about the worries of Channel 4 about the IBA's attitude; don't forget the support that the IBA was giving you at this time, both generally speaking and in particular over the *Scum* case.[49] Now that is not impartiality, but is something that is a significant measure of support.

Tusa: I think that we should draw it to a close. I just wonder if there is one final thought that each one of you would like to have before we wind up?

Smith: I would like to say that I would hate future historians to think that a rift between Jeremy and Edmund was a major issue in the early years of Channel 4. This was not the case. I think that Edmund has become much crosser about it in recent years. That is my feeling, and also I must say that there was one day when we met in the room before Jeremy was appointed, when Edmund said with his usual acerbic wit, 'I am the only person in this room that has never heard of Jeremy Isaacs.' And the fact was that everybody else had. It wasn't a clique that pushed Jeremy onto Edmund. It was that in the preceding months the whole world of broadcasting in Britain had been a-buzz about Channel 4 and who would run it, and Jeremy had become inevitable. It was obvious that was the way that the Channel was going, towards the particular gifts that this outstanding personality possessed. Edmund wasn't involved at that time, and therefore it did seem to him when he was Chairman that this character was being propelled towards him. I don't think that really was what was happening.

Tusa: Jeremy, your final thought, and then Edmund to round off.

Isaacs: Well, it is a pity that we have run out of time because there is a great deal else to say, especially Justin Dukes' role in fixing the level of ITV subscription to the upper end of the parameters that Brian Young had offered us, and can I just say that if I had had the kind of funding [at the Royal Opera House] that I had at Channel 4, I would be a happier man.

Tusa: Edmund, it was your very candid paper which really began this whole seminar. How do you put together what you wrote in your paper and what you said in this seminar?

Dell: Well, I'm very grateful, as I often was as Chairman of the Board, to Tony Smith whose contributions to the Board I always thought were remarkable. As to the rift between Jeremy and me, there was a disagreement about current affairs, but the relationship, I thought most of the time on most subjects, was actually rather co-operative.

Isaacs: It was. When I said what I said at your last meeting Edmund, it wasn't bunkum, it was true.

Dell: That I represented in my paper. I was therefore astonished when

Witness Seminar

not I, not angry Dell, but apparently angry Isaacs, published a book full of inaccuracies,[50] which was in all essential respects an attack on the Chairman with whom I thought relations had become after a difficult beginning rather good. Now, I am not angry, I am delighted at Channel 4. I am delighted at its subsequent success. I wish that we had not actually run out of time because there are many things we could have actually usefully discussed about the relations of a thing like Channel 4 with a regulatory authority, and actually I have to say that I was more deeply concerned about that relationship than about the relationship between Jeremy and me, because with this exception – aside from the point of current affairs – I had thought Jeremy and I had worked out a way of living together.

Tusa: I should thank those that have taken part. I apologise for not dipping sufficiently deeply into the knowledge and historical experience of the others, but I will be very surprised if this text does not become an absolutely basic text for an important part of the history of television of the last 15 to 20 years.

ACKNOWLEDGEMENT

The Institute of Contemporary British History gratefully acknowledges the generous support of Channel 4 Television in making this seminar possible.

NOTES

1. Sir Harry Pilkington (chairman), *Report of the Committee on Broadcasting*, Cmnd 1753, 1961.
2. All of Anthony Smith's material relating to Channel 4, including his various articles for *The Guardian*, has been deposited at the National Film and Television Archive, London.
3. Lord Annan (chairman), *Report of the Committee on the Future of Broadcasting*, Cmnd 6753, 1977.
4. Editor of *This Week*, Thames Television, 1967–70; Labour MP, Derby North, 1970–83; member of the Annan Committee, 1974–77.
5. *Broadcasting*, Cmnd 7294, 1978, especially pp.10–13.
6. David Doherty, David E Morrison and Michael Tracey, *Keeping Faith? Channel Four and its Audience* (London: John Libbey, 1988), p.23.
7. *Daily Mail*, 22 October 1984.
8. She also was by then apparently convinced, though senior colleagues were not, that Channel 4 ought to handle its own advertising; see Tom O'Malley, *Closedown? The*

BBC and Government Broadcasting Policy 1979–92 (London: Pluto, 1994), pp.68, 82.
9. Alan Peacock (chairman), *Report of the Committee on Financing the British Broadcasting Corporation*, Cmnd 9824, 1986, recommendation 14, p.144.
10. *Broadcasting in the 90s: Competition, Choice and Quality. The Government's plans for broadcasting legislation*, Cm 517, 1988.
11. Doherty *et al.*, p.176.
12. Whitelaw indeed told the Royal Television Society, 'Competitive advertising on the two channels would inevitably result in a move towards single-minded concentration on maximising the audience for audiences' sake,' quoted in *Independent Broadcasting Authority Annual Report and Accounts 1979–80*, p.140.
13. Sir Robert Fraser, first Director-General, Independent Television Authority, 1954–70; Chairman, ITN, 1971–74. The two deputies were Bernard Sendall and Anthony Pragnell.
14. See Simon Blanchard and David Morley (eds), *What's This Channel Four?* (London: Comedia, 1982), p.8.
15. Minister of Posts and Telecommunications, 1972–74.
16. Conservative MP 1959–64, 1974–97; Vice Chairman of the Conservatives' Broadcasting Committee, 1975.
17. Head of Current Affairs, LWT 1977–81; Director of Programmes, 1982–87; Deputy Director-General BBC, 1987–92; BBC Director-General, 1992–.
18. Presenter, *Weekend World*, 1972–77; Ambassador to the USA, 1977–79; Chairman and Chief Executive, TV-AM, 1980–83; presenter, *A Week in Politics*, Channel 4, 1983–86.
19. Producer, Thames Television, 1972–82; Founder, Brook Productions 1982; Director of Programmes, Thames Television, 1986–92.
20. A reference to Roy Thomson's famous comment in about 1957, shortly after he set up STV, 'It's just like having a licence to print your own money!' cited in Russell Braddon, *Roy Thomson of Fleet Street* (London: Collins, 1965), p.240.
21. For a discussion of a particular example of the effect of this in practice see Peter Catterall (ed.), 'Reassessing the Impact of *Yesterday's Men*', *Contemporary British History*, Vol.10, No.4, 1997, p.122.
22. On 27 August 1979 in Edinburgh, reproduced in abridged form in *The Listener*, 6 September 1979, pp.298–300.
23. Journalist, *The Guardian*, 1978–81; Senior Commissioning Editor, Channel 4, 1981–88; Director of Programmes, 1988–93.
24. Senior Commissioning Editor, Channel 4, 1981–88; head of drama, 1988–90.
25. Director, Channel 4, 1980–84.
26. Director, Channel 4, 1981–85.
27. A reference to Sir John Eden.
28. Conservative MP, 1959–64, 1966–74.
29. Vice-Chairman, Conservative Party, 1971–75; Director, Channel 4, 1980–85. On the committee and the Conservatives see also Stephen Lambert, *Channel 4: Television with a Difference* (London: BFI Publishing, 1982), p.64.
30. The Channel 4 Board, when established, was reasonably balanced between Labour and Conservative. Ironically appointees from both sides of the political fence, including Morrison and Smith, tended in the early 1980s to gravitate towards the SDP.
31. A producer who later worked for Channel 4.
32. A television talks producer appointed as secretary to the 'Unthinkable Committee' set

Witness Seminar

up by the BBC to look into the worst possible scenarios which might emerge from the Annan Committee. 'Deflecting pressure from the ITV companies for a second channel in their hands was one of the Committee's prime concerns,' letter by Colin Shaw to Peter Catterall, 2 May 1997. See also profile of Michael Starks in *Ariel*, 13 May 1997, p.9.

33. Robin Day, *Television: A Personal Account* (London: Hutchinson, 1961), ch.14.
34. 1970–72.
35. *The Guardian*, 21 April 1972.
36. Association of Cinematograph, Television and Allied Technicians.
37. John Ranelagh was a commissioning editor at Channel 4, 1981–88 and Secretary to the Board 1981–83. The text of his letter is published elsewhere in this volume.
38. Controller, BBC2, 1978–82; Director of Programmes, BBC television, 1983–85; Managing Director, BBC Radio, 1985–87.
39. Senior Commissioning Editor, Educational Programmes, Channel 4, 1981–89. On these appointments see Jeremy Isaacs, *Storm over 4* (London: Weidenfeld & Nicolson, 1989), pp.35–8.
40. Governor, BBC, 1970–75; Chairman, IBA, 1975–80.
41. On Channel 4's educational output see Naomi Sargant, *Adult Learners, Broadcasting and Channel 4* (London: Channel 4 Television, 1992).
42. But see Naomi Sargant's contribution to this volume.
43. The Kensington House Group was a group of BBC producers in the 1960s and 1970s. It incurred the wrath of Huw Wheldon, the then Managing Director, Television, over its submission to the Annan Committee. Its suggestions included the idea of separating production and broadcasting functions (in the manner subsequently followed in Channel 4) and the introduction of producer choice in relation to facilities: letter to Peter Catterall from Paul Bonner, 23 April 1997, enclosing his 'A View from the Other Side'.
44. Lord Thomson of Monifieth, Chairman of the IBA, 1981–88.
45. See Blanchard and Morley; Doherty *et al.*, p.29f. Naomi Sargant's view, from within the commissioning process, was 'Up to a point'.
46. Strictly speaking it would be more correct to say that IBT, led by Ann Zamu, bombarded Channel 4, initially Liz Forgan and then Naomi Sargant as education commissioning editor, with demands for programme slots, only some of which were met.
47. Director-General, IBA, 1982–89.
48. Sir James Hamilton.
49. A reference to the controversial film shown on Channel 4 on 10 June 1983. The decision of the IBA to allow this broadcast suffered an unsuccessful legal challenge by Mary Whitehouse, see Isaacs, pp.116–18.
50. A reference to Isaacs' memoir, *op. cit.*

Channel 4: News and Current Affairs 1981–87

LIZ FORGAN

Catterall: Firstly can you tell me how you came to be a senior commissioning editor of Channel 4?

Forgan: The story [people tell] is true. I was the woman's editor of *The Guardian*, it was the summer, all my columnists had gone on holiday simultaneously, *The Guardian* was too poor to pay any substitutes so I had to write all their columns myself. I did a series called 'Women and the Media Men', in which I interviewed people in grand media organisations, including Jeremy Isaacs who at that moment had just been declared head of this newly announced channel. So I wrote him a letter saying are you aware that you are the great white hope of 51 per cent of the population who feel themselves completely traduced by television, please can I have an early interview. He said yes, and I went round to where they were at that time camped out on the roof of the IBA at Brompton Towers in Knightsbridge, and I did a long interview with him all about what he thought of his channel and women. He was, as he always is, articulate, original, amusing and right. At the end I said that it sounds absolutely wonderful, I wish you all the very best, thank you for a marvellous interview, turned off my tape recorder, and he said, would you like to come and help me run it. I said, do you realise that I never watch television, I'm a print journalist, I hate television, I loath and despise it, it's a poisonous medium about which I know and care nothing. Perfect, he said, just what I want. He said that he was really looking for people who did not come with television

---

This interview was conducted by Peter Catterall on 20 July 1998.

News and Current Affairs

training and prejudices. This was an extraordinary opportunity to do something different. The only way to do that was to mix in with people like himself, who had spent their lives in television, other people who had expertise in other directions.

Catterall: Presumably you had not met Jeremy beforehand?

Forgan: I think I had met him once at a party. I came, I suppose, with the average liberal newspaper journalist's prejudices. I believed in pluralism of expression, I believed that the media ought to be simply channels to allow the expression of all sorts of points of view. Obviously the organ itself, in the case of a newspaper, would take an attitude. But one of the essential jobs of a reporter is to convey into the public domain the thoughts, the ideas, the attitudes, the events that are happening in our society so that people have a means of knowing what is going on around them. That is actually a very different attitude to the media from the one which on the whole prevailed in television at the time, which was all about a very heavily regulated industry. I think that television journalists – at that time and still – operated with a tremendous built-in sense of worry about the rules governing impartiality. I think that a lot of people thought that I in particular and the Channel in general had a careless attitude to fairness, that we were a bunch of lefties with an agenda, determined to push a point of view and suppress another one. Nothing could be further from the truth. What we were after was arriving at fairness in broadcasting by almost the opposite direction from the normal one, i.e. publish everything, rather than only publishing a really very narrow accepted agenda from half-left to half-right, which was the prevailing fare on television at the time.

Catterall: Absolutely everything?

Forgan: Not everything, certainly not. But this was a four channel environment we were talking about. I think it is very important to remember quite what a restricted television environment Channel 4 was born into. Even now, before digital has really hit, the situation is transformed. In those days on the three existing channels the available spectrum of journalism was extremely narrow. That's the overriding reason why the early days of Channel 4 were marked as a sort of mad,

The Making of Channel 4

anarchist, left-wing explosion. All that, black people, sexual politics, was completely unrepresented and kept off the agenda. Channel 4 brought it right into the mainstream, and I think that caused a tremendous skew initially in its agenda and the way it was looked at. But I absolutely resist the idea that it was a leftie operation.

As an example I would point to something that drove Edmund Dell crackers, the first stream of real radical Thatcherite thinking that ever got on to British television was on Channel 4 through *Diverse Reports* and through *The New Enlightenment*, which I commissioned. I thought that arguments always became boring if you simply had Mr Black and Mr White debating, they always got stuck on the second paragraph. If you really wanted to get into the bones of an argument you had to have Mr White, Ms Off-White, Mr Grey and Mrs Dazzling White, and then you could have something interesting. So we had this series of programmes which was all people on the right debating the way the New Right was emerging. If you looked at the horizon of British political thinking and activity at that moment, that was the moving point and that's where television should have been, and that's where we were, regardless of the fact that it happened to be on the right of the spectrum. When there was an item on the privatisation of prisons Edmund Dell said this was so unthinkable that it must have been just an attempt to discredit the right. Three years later it was government policy. But this shows that we were not just a bunch of old 1960s lefties going on about nuclear weapons – we were, some of the time, but by no means exclusively.

At first the idea was that we would do almost nothing ourselves. My first brief was to be commissioning editor for news, current affairs, documentaries, sport and the arts, on the grounds that all the commissioning editor was supposed to do was just pick the people, agree what they were going to do, make sure they did not break the law, and put it on the air. The history of Channel 4 from day one to today has been of a steady erosion of that principle, mainly on the grounds of quality control, but also on other grounds too, not least that the people in possession in broadcasting simply cannot hand it over to someone else without sticking their fingers in it.

Catterall: But also, of course, you didn't have a proprietorial interest.

Forgan: That was part of the point about getting people who didn't

News and Current Affairs

know about television. I couldn't make programmes better than they could, and I knew it, so I didn't have the temptation to go and sit in people's cutting rooms all day. That was part of Jeremy's plan. He wanted people who lacked the craft and couldn't be tempted to make the programmes instead of the people whose job it was.

Catterall: But a number of the early programmes lacked the craft...

Forgan: They were terrible. We put some appalling programmes on the air. Never mind my lack of television experience, it was perfectly obvious to me as it was to everyone else that they were, and not just in the technical sense, appalling. They were long and rambling, they were badly made, they were undisciplined, they were sometimes unfair and sometimes inarticulate, but what they never were was a waste of this precious gift that Parliament had given us: the money, the airtime and the job to do something different. It may be that we were indulged a bit too long, but if you really want to break the mould, that's what you have to do.

Catterall: Before Channel 4, when controversial programmes were made there usually seems to have been an attempt at a balancing item. Was there pressure to do that on Channel 4 as well?

Forgan: Yes. One of my main jobs at Channel 4 was to indulge in a ten-year-long negotiation with the IBA to renegotiate the terms of what you mean by balance in television. That whole argument rested on the idea that if you were adding another channel you were also adding a little bit more latitude. I arrived at a rough tariff with the ITC (as the IBA became). I said that there were grades of impartiality that demand different responses. If you call an individual person by name a murderer, then you must immediately allow him personally to defend himself. If you say that the government is a bunch of scoundrels you should within a decent interval in a mature democracy provide an opportunity for them to address that. If you simply say 'the world is arranged in such a way and we ought to think about arranging it differently', you can take your time about broadcasting an opposite view. As the picture gets bigger and bigger and more and more remote from individual harm, so in an educated liberal democracy with a thriving press and four television channels there is room for your balance to spread over a longer and longer timeframe; it is not appropriate to apply the same rules of balance to every kind of polemical statement. Over the years we worked out a decent approach to that. So, with *The New Enlightenment*, I was allowed to run an entire series whose agenda was to the right of centre, nobody to the left of centre even appeared. But the rationale was accepted, it was a serious attempt to engage with an important stream of current political argument. Had it been on the left I doubt if we would have got away with it.

We played the same game in different ways. *The Friday Alternative* went week and week about, with one week someone saying nuclear energy is dangerous and the next week someone else saying privatise prisons. I would argue that this represented a stroke for the left and a stroke for the right, despite the fact that they did not address each other's arguments. It's an insulting way to try and create balance, but sometimes that's what you had to do to make sure you were complying with the law. My own private morality said that we should never leave the audience in ignorance of any important or relevant strand of a given argument. But, with that in mind, it was important for television to grow up and allow that incredible medium of public information to be used for sharp polemical or personal views in the way that print could be used.

Catterall: Having come at it from a print background, did you feel that television had limitations in terms of journalism?

Forgan: Yes it did. When I decided to leave newspapers and go into the hated television I did it because I thought it would be huge fun, but also because television was the most powerful medium of our time. I thought it was extremely important that the conventional wisdom that television could not be used for ideas or serious thinking of any sort had to be challenged. That's why we did *Channel 4 News*. I went to ITN one day to explain to them what it was we had in mind. We wanted an hour-long news programme, a third of the programme to be foreign affairs, a specialist economics correspondent, no sport, no stories about the Royal Family, no crime and no pictures of black limousines drawing up outside unidentifiable buildings and driving away again. There was a sharp intake of breath and then a very senior member of the Board said to me, 'Well my dear' – which was a mistake

News and Current Affairs

on his part – 'you haven't been in television very long and there's one thing you have to understand: the news is the news is the news.' I said that if there was one single phrase that most sums up what I did not want to do with *Channel 4 News* it was that. You can see in the early editions of *Channel 4 News* what a disaster it was. We had Sarah Hogg, who was a wonderful economics journalist, but she cannot do television to save her life. She sat there looking at the camera like a threatened rabbit and it was a catastrophe. The set was ghastly, we were not having desks so the scripts all fell on the floor, the programme maundered on and on without a beginning or end and there weren't any viewers. Every now and then you can see a glimpse of what it might be. Then came the miners' strike in 1984–85. All of a sudden we had time to get past the first minute and thirty seconds of the argument in which somebody snarls at somebody else or there's a shot of pickets or whatever, and we forced them to talk. Then you see how transforming it is to move television away from incident to explanation.

Jeremy Isaacs had had this idea for a long time, but it immediately echoed what I thought about journalism. We wrote the prospectus for this and hawked it round.

Catterall: So did you have to go to ITN?

Forgan: No. There may have been some deal, but I never knew about it. As I remember it, a number of people pitched for this business, including LWT who at the time were producing the best current affairs programme on television, *Weekend World*. Barry Cox and John Birt pitched their vision of this hour-long news to me, and they prepared it immaculately. They described what in many ways would have been the apotheosis of John's vision of broadcasting, but it wasn't mine. It was a long, theoretical and analytical current affairs programme, and I wanted a news programme with brains, I didn't want a lecture with pictures. So at the end I had to say thank you but I'm going to give the contract to ITN because I think that we can work with ITN's energy and brilliant news sense and force them to import some thinking and analysis, but I think that you will squash the life out of it. It was a bit of a thing to say, here was I, Miss No-one from nowhere telling this to the greatest bunch of journalists in British television at the time. However, about three weeks later I got a telephone call from John Birt inviting me for lunch. So, with my knees knocking slightly, I went. He said that he thought I had made the wrong decision and that they would have done the programme better, but that he wanted me to know that that was now water under the bridge. Channel 4 was the most important thing to have happened in British television in his lifetime and he would do anything to help it or me personally. I think that was pretty splendid after I had just turned down his idea.

Catterall: Do you think you had problems of credibility...

Forgan: Certainly, but in a funny way I think it helped. I was blissfully unaware of the enormity of what I was saying, because I'd been brought up in print journalism and all these ideas were not extraordinary to me at all. But I was so outside the mould for them.

Catterall: With this background on *The Guardian*'s women's page, how far did you try to import a women's angle to Channel 4? How far were you bringing in something to a man's world?

Forgan: There were two aspects to that. One was the actual body of people who made up Channel 4 itself. It was absolutely clear that Jeremy was determined to have a proper balance between men and women in his channel. I think frankly that one of the reasons that he made me head of news and current affairs was that he thought having a woman as head of journalism would be a very clear sign of what he was about. There were three senior commissioning editors, two of whom were women. That was a very strong signal in terms of television at the time. The commissioning body then grew up, and it was a fair mix. It felt different from the average television company. I hadn't realised quite how different until in the very early days of the Channel, Paul Bonner, Ellis Griffiths (the chief engineer) and I constituted ourselves as a little embassy and went round all the ITV companies. We'd go on the train to wherever it was and we'd be ushered into the board room and we'd have coffee with the key people before looking around the company. In every single case except one, when we went in there was a big shiny table and a dozen men in suits around it. I was always the only woman except for the person pouring the coffee, except at Tyne Tees, where Andrea Wonfor was a senior executive. Jeremy decided that Channel 4 was not going to be like that, so in all sorts of places where you wouldn't expect it there were women. That had one very important effect, which is that you didn't start off with the automatic filtering prejudices that come from having only men deciding whether something is interesting or not.

At the beginning there was only one piece of conscious feminist experimentation, and that was in my decision to commission our key weekly current affairs programme from two independent production companies, both of which were run, and one of which was exclusively staffed, by women. Broadside was the feminist collective, whilst 20/20 Vision, which is still going, was run by two extremely good women, but certainly employed men. The reason why I did this was simply to test the proposition that women would look at current affairs in a different way from the teams of men that were currently producing *World in Action* or *Panorama*.

This went on for a year or so with the whole of that strand commissioned from those two companies. The most important difference we detected was in the witnesses they called. Many more women contributed to those programmes. In some senses the agenda was different. But, on the whole, not much difference.

Catterall: But you didn't try and commission anything specifically for women?

Forgan: I never believed in commissioning programmes for women. In fact when I was at *The Guardian*'s women's page we used to have an argument every year about whether we should go on having a women's page. Sometimes I argued for it, and sometimes I argued against it. But on the whole I never did believe in programmes for women. I believed in programmes by women or about women, but programmes *for* women – what do you mean?

Catterall: How much freedom of action did you have?

Forgan: Complete freedom of action, too much in fact. I didn't have a plan at all at the beginning and I was just overwhelmed with the sense of responsibility to keep the door open to all the ideas coming in as long as we could. It was clear that it would have to start shutting eventually if we were to get a sensible channel on the air, but the sense of the release of energy and hope and excitement that Channel 4 started is hard for people to remember now. I sat in my room with my door opening and shutting every 15 minutes, and through it paraded a million people. I didn't know any of them from a bar of soap. So much did I not know them that I couldn't tell if the next person due was the latest BAFTA award-winning Rembrandt of British television or some scalliwag off the street, and I had 15 minutes to make up my mind.

I said to Jeremy one day, 'Look, this is terribly dangerous. I'm making decisions on pure instinct. Why don't I tell you who's coming to see me and then you can tell me who are the really good filmmakers.' He said to me, 'Certainly not, the whole point of hiring somebody without any experience is that you will make those decisions all over again.' That is an example of how really courageous Jeremy's commitment to innovation was. If you really want to innovate, the person at the very top of the organisation has to take the risk, with the certainty of some failure. Jeremy refused to insure against my inexperience in all the ways that were available to him. He refused to provide any safety nets except himself, and he took the rap for all of this. I think it's probably a completely unique example in the history of British television of someone taking that sort of risk for the sake of opening the doors and letting new voices be heard. That is now the platitudinous grammar of all television. Nobody begins to do it the way that Jeremy did at the start of Channel 4. And it only emerged later – I wasn't on the Board then – what blows were raining down on his back.

Catterall: How much do you think you got it right?

Forgan: I think we got it quite a lot right. Some of the people who made programmes for Channel 4 in the early days never made a good television programme, but they got onto that screen something real and extraordinary and something that you simply don't get from well-made product. I'm older and wiser now and I like polished television, but every now and again something happens which isn't supposed to and you see truth. I think we did a lot of that on Channel 4, as well as finding some real talent of course.

I remember the first encounter between the Board and the commissioning editors. I was personally cocooned in my inexperience and had no idea what a terrible thing we were doing. I just thought it was an interesting experiment. But I think that the ITV directors who were on the Board at the beginning deserve a lot of credit. They

News and Current Affairs

thought catering for minority interests meant badminton or West Indian cooking, they did not think it meant all this rambling, politically difficult, often technically awful programmes. But they hung on and came to see the point.

Catterall: Like IBT?

Forgan: Well, IBT was comparatively well organised, although it was Third Worldy and very angry. But certainly in terms of an appeal to a British audience, absolutely zero. I think Jeremy banned ratings books from the Channel for at least the first year, I don't think we had a clue what the audiences were. I knew that the audiences for *Channel 4 News* were almost non-existent, but we all thought that was only to be expected. The brilliant formula that Whitelaw had come up with separated the people making the editorial decisions from those responsible for generating the income. In less brilliant hands than Jeremy's it could have been a recipe for a really shocking waste of money, but it was the way to get done the job they declared they wanted doing: a new breath of air and new thinking on British television. The ITV directors were the people who were responsible to the grown-ups back at the ITV companies who were selling the air-time for these ghastly programmes, each one of which outraged the advertisers and the readers of the *Daily Mail* more. What's more, we had a policy which completely went against the traditional policy of building an audience through an evening. You would have a programme aimed at former permanent under-secretaries one minute, followed by a rant from some community group the next. Every time a programme ended the whole of the audience went with it. It was, in commercial terms, a disaster.

Catterall: Did you have any input into scheduling?

Forgan: No. But it was fine for us because we were having the fun of it and not any of the responsibility. The people who had the responsibility did keep their nerve, and I would say that Bill Brown in particular, Brian Tesler too, although he was pretty fierce with us, and Paul Fox were pretty heroic in those early days.

Catterall: Presumably you had some kind of relationship with the ITV companies as well through the commissioning process?

Forgan: Yes, and that was a bit tricky too, mainly because they thought, not unreasonably, that we just had to let them know what we wanted and they'd deliver it.

We wanted to treat them like independent producers, which was unrealistic on our part. But we fought our way to a decent relationship. In particular there was a relationship with Central, which was very interesting and difficult. Central took a different view to the other ITV companies. They tried to think what it was that we wanted, which was an intelligent thing to do, but they gave us two things which caused us enormous problems. One was a series about the trade union movement made by Ken Loach, and the second was a science programme called *Crucible*. The science programme was just not very good, and I didn't handle it very well. It wasn't very good science, it was very angry and political and it didn't impress the scientific community at all, let alone anyone else.

The Ken Loach series was, I think, a defining moment for the Channel, especially with Edmund. It was a series of programmes called *Questions of Leadership*, and it was at the moment when there was a big challenge in the trade movement to an ageing cadre of moderate to right-wing leaders, in which Ken was an active participant. And he made these brilliant programmes which made trade union life just spring out of the screen, you could hear those green canvas chairs being stacked after meetings, it was close, close, close. But it wasn't just the Frank Chapples and the Moss Evanses who were in the firing line but the whole trade union leadership, and selling out the working class was the story. Ken was grinding his own axes, which I could see was a bit of a problem. I thought it was important we got it on the screen because nobody has ever communicated so clearly what being in a trade union was like. But as it stood we couldn't transmit it, it was just too unfair. Edmund had somehow managed to see the fine cuts and was terribly upset. So I went to the TUC and spent a week drinking more whisky than I have ever drunk in my life trying to persuade the leaders of the trade union movement to take part in a final programme in which they would be given a decent chance to have their say. They were not keen to do this because they were gambling on the notion that if they refused to take part we would be unable to transmit the series. In the end I persuaded four big trade union leaders to take part and I got back to the Channel triumphant, only to find that Edmund had returned the whole series to Central.

News and Current Affairs

The Board of Central then decided they would not 'officially' submit them to Channel 4, and they were never transmitted, which I think was a shame. Ken then set his children to write me pitiful letters asking why had I been so beastly to their daddy! But the Channel should have transmitted that series along with a balancing programme, and I blame Edmund for that.

The Board actually intervened very rarely, but Edmund had obviously identified the factual area as one that he was concerned about. The deal in any sensible television company (and Channel 4 settled quite quickly into this mode) was that the Board said to its executives, 'These are the rules, we expect you to follow them, and we expect you to alert us to anything that is likely to cause a hoo-hah, but on the whole we won't watch anything before transmission unless you ask us to.' That, I think, is now a written policy, and I had something to do with making it so, but it became the *de facto* policy of the Board quite early on. The Board should not be taken by surprise by reading in the newspapers of some terrible row. On the other hand, they need to be another regulatory and supervisory layer, not part of the executive decision-making.

Catterall: But if you had problems with the Board, you didn't have problems with politicians?

Forgan: A lot of politicians thought we were terrible and there were constant rows. My way of dealing with them was to get them on television. That's why I started *Right to Reply*. I never could see the point of having quiet little rows at the IBA. The people who needed to know if someone ought to be rebuked were the viewers. So we started this programme, which I think is the way complaints ought to be dealt with on television. If you had a complaint you were invited onto a programme where you could stay the whole day at the Channel if you wanted to, you had someone to help you compile your argument, you had a chairman who was the best current affairs journalist I could find in the business, Gus MacDonald, whose job was not to be a neutral chairman but to be on the side of the complainant. The complainant had the last word, and we produced the person about whose work they were complaining to sit across the table and talk about the complaint. If some viewer thinks there is a point of view which wasn't properly represented, let them represent it, and let the viewers make their own minds up.

Catterall: This raises again this point about whether television tends to present matters in black and white.

Forgan: I don't think that's right. If you think of the miners' strike, the Channel 4 journalists just grew in stature as that went on. They thought of more and more brilliant ways of using television to pull out the arguments, the feelings, the history, because they had this time to fill.

The Channel also quickly began to have an effect on other broadcasters. I remember having a conversation with a senior BBC current affairs executive which shocked me to my bootstraps shortly after Channel 4 began. One of the gaps we had identified was that there were no domestic political programmes on British television at the time at all. I thought that was extraordinary, so we started *A Week in Politics*. Immediately the BBC then started an equal and opposite programme. And I said to this BBC executive, 'I'm just thinking whether to recommission *A Week in Politics*, now you've started to do the job it's not strictly necessary for us,' (at that time my policy was simply to do what wasn't being done elsewhere). 'For God's sake, don't do that,' he said, 'we only put it there because you do *A Week in Politics*.' I found this shocking. For the BBC to spend its licence money in this way I thought was scandalous.

The injection of argument rather than just opinions, the admission to the screen of numbers of black people and Asians, *The Tube* making *Top of the Pops* look like a vicarage tea party, and the new deal with the film business through *Film on Four*, some marvellous drama – in all those ways Channel 4 did completely shake up British television. I don't think the mistakes matter. We are forgiven for the mistakes. What we would never have been forgiven for was not using that amazing brief and funding system to do something different.

Catterall: But how much was what you did your idea and how much was it these people beating a path to your door?

Forgan: I think the balance moved. At the beginning I tried very hard to have a self-denying ordinance and not to decide what I wanted and then go and look for it. The first job was to release all this squashed down creative energy and see what was there. There were just a few things I knew we had to do – *Channel 4 News*, *A Week in Politics*, *Right* *to Reply* and this experiment with women. Other than that there was absolutely no prescription. I think that over the years the balance has completely gone the other way. The Channel now decides what jobs it wants doing where. Even the independent producers like it better that way.

Maybe people will look upon the early years of Channel 4 as a ridiculous piece of Pollyanna nonsense only made possible by an extremely privileged situation where we didn't have to worry about where the money came from. Indeed it was. The question is, did British television and the audience get something back in return, and I think the answer is yes. If Channel 4 had been the first television channel you wouldn't have started it like that, but it was the fourth one and it needed to break new ground.

Catterall: Were you ever under any pressure to accept more from ITV companies?

Forgan: Yes. Not serious pressure. There used to be elaborate arguments as to how much subscription Scotland was paying and how few commissions were going to Scotland, but the answer was always the same: give us stronger, more exciting programmes. There were no quotas.

The great benefit of having people like me at the beginning was I absolutely believed the rhetoric. I can remember a conversation with David Elstein, then at Brook Productions, in which he was incredulous when I told him that I might take a show like *A Week in Politics* off the air whilst it was still successful, simply and only because it was time for a change. But the principal objective was to keep the oxygen coming in, and to do that you not only have to chuck out unsuccessful shows but some successful ones as well. That was all fairy dust really, but I believed in it. You couldn't go on running a channel like that, but at the beginning it was right. Inevitably in time you are drawn into competing for audiences, and to do that you have to do things that are absolutely inimical to innovation. Continuity becomes important. The best way to keep an audience is to keep the people who already like it.

There was a hilarious discussion early in the Channel when we were thinking very seriously about how we were going to fulfil this obligation to all these assorted people and how we were ever going to be able to market ourselves to anybody, and Jeremy said that what we should do was that at the end of every programme the presenter's voice should come on and say 'If you liked that last programme you will hate the next one so why don't you go out and play tennis'. It was only half a joke!

Catterall: But are we talking about something which had ceased to be so innovative by the mid-1980s?

Forgan: I think it actually continued to be seriously innovative. It obviously settled down from its early hysteria and threw out some of the more extreme pursuits. When was its apogee? I don't know, maybe about six years in. But then it changed and got excellent in different ways. I think it had a job to do which was absolutely of the moment. It rightly saw that life then changed and it changed with it. The extraordinary thing, for which we should all thank the good Lord on our knees, was that an extraordinary government idea, a brilliant funding formula and the absolutely perfect person to run it came together in a magic moment. It was the best fun to work on that I've ever had and I think everyone who was there at the beginning feels the same.

Catterall: This point about the funding formula raises the Peacock recommendations and the question of the Channel selling its own airtime, which would increase audience pressure. Was this something you as commissioning editors were insulated from?

Forgan: No. We all joined in all of those discussions. We were all absolutely determined that if Channel 4 had to sell its own airtime it would not change its nature, but of course it did. You become responsible and professional, and the ability to try things and not think about the consequences in terms of ratings and income disappears if you are selling your own airtime. Now, you could argue that at the time Channel 4 finally did get to sell its own airtime that was the right thing to do. You can't be a child forever. But Peacock was too soon. The Channel needed to play for longer to grow up properly. I still think it would be rather fun to have a channel that didn't have to sell its own airtime. I certainly think you would have to sack all the people who ran it and start again from time to time. We did have this rule on Channel 4 that you would turn over the whole of the commissioning body every

News and Current Affairs

ten years, so that no-one would ever get settled. Michael Grade[1] thought that was completely mad. If you've got hold of a good executive what on earth are you doing firing them, and in professional terms he's right. But if your real strategic objective is innovation that's what you have to do. That's why when the Channel 4 job came up[2] I refused to put my name forward because when I think about Channel 4 I think about how it was in the 1980s.

Catterall: Did you ever have overlaps or conflicts with the other commissioning editors?

Forgan: Not very often because the Channel was then run on the basis that no-one had a deputy, everyone did their own thing and the only person who ran everybody was Jeremy. So I didn't have any reporting structure around me, nor did any of my colleagues. That has now changed, it's now got hierarchical like everywhere else. Indeed when I became Director of Programmes there was huge pressure to do that then. I said to everyone, 'no deputies, if you've got too much work chop off a bit of your job and give it to somebody else'. You can have people who cover for you when you are away, but they must have a job of their own. No hierarchy.

I can remember two sorts of ideological quarrels that we used to have. John Ranelagh at every programme review board would make a speech about how nobody but him understood the need for proper intellectual rigour and impartiality. He and I would quarrel a lot because he thought I was a dangerous leftie, which was complete nonsense.

And I can think of one really serious quarrel with almost all my colleagues about whether we should carry the National Front election broadcasts in 1983. They said that we were the Channel who said to the black community: 'here is your voice', we could not therefore have these people on our screens. I replied that we were a pluralist channel in a democracy, they were standing in an election and we must have them on our screens. I won, but my punishment was to appear on *Right to Reply* (which I was the editor of). The experience just proved to me what a good programme it was. To be confronted by a schoolteacher, a fantastically articulate black schoolboy and a quiet black woman, all personally outraged and offended by what I done. It really made you, as a producer, understand the consequences of your actions. It didn't surprise me, but it really brought it home.

Catterall: Were the changes in the nature of the output of your own volition? Were you ever under any pressure from the Board?

Forgan: We didn't feel pressures from anywhere at the beginning. The newspapers used to slag us off all the time and our colleagues in professional television used to sneer from time to time, but we had such an adrenalin buzz that we paid no attention. What went on at the Board simply never came near any of us as commissioning editors. Later I became Director of Programmes and joined the Board myself, but by-and-large it was an exceptionally supportive and courageous body which thought its primary duty was to keep its nerve and protect the programme makers.

Catterall: Jeremy Isaacs insulated you from all that?

Forgan: Absolutely. Jeremy was either very clever and chose people who would mirror his own approach, or he was serious about pluralism. I only had one serious row with Jeremy. That was over *Right to Reply*. Suddenly his instincts for innovation completely deserted him and he became a traditional television producer. 'How can you expose these shy, creative people in this way?' My view was that television producers are highly paid and enormously privileged people whose work comes into everyone's sitting room, and the least they can do is to sit still and be accountable to the viewers on television themselves. He never ever bought that view. I put him on the programme himself twice. Both times he behaved abominably. He lost his temper with a viewer making a perfectly legitimate point and fired me (we made it up afterwards). He really thought that was the wrong thing to do, but he didn't stop me doing it. He genuinely thought producers should be sheltered. I didn't.

Catterall: I suppose the argument was that producers might become less creative if they are exposed in this way?

Forgan: Yes, a nonsensical argument.

I suppose one could envisage a television channel which did much more radical things. I don't think you could in those days. Interactivity will make a whole different story.

I think the job then was to do something different, to shake up the

News and Current Affairs

agenda and the cast of people who made television. That was the real strategic challenge that was set for the Channel and I think that's what we did.

NOTES

1. Jeremy Isaacs' successor as Chief Executive of Channel 4.
2. To succeed Michael Grade in 1997.

Channel 4:
The Educational Output 1981–89

NAOMI SARGANT

Catterall: Perhaps you could start off by telling me how you came to be appointed to Channel 4.

Sargant: I'd been working at the Open University for about 11 years; I ran the survey research department and then became Pro-Vice Chancellor in charge of student affairs. Then under the 1974–79 Labour government I was appointed to the Advisory Committee for Adult and Continuing Education, which was chaired by Richard Hoggart, and was given the task of chairing the group which did the planning nationally for continuing education. So I had been setting out a structure of opportunities of education for adults as a process continuing throughout life. Related to that I had been part of and commissioned a major study of education and leisure interests amongst adults, and that is the context in which I think Jeremy [Isaacs] thought I would be appropriate for the job.

Catterall: So he contacted you?

Sargant: Well, we knew each other, but that went back 20 years or so. I had always been very admiring of his work, for example *The World at War*. We had shared a number of friends and we had frequently discussed the educational power of television. I remember us discussing the educational effect of *The World at War*. He said, 'I suppose you think that *The World at War* isn't educational.' I said,

---

This interview was conducted by Peter Catterall on 30 July 1998.

The Educational Output

'Nonsense, of course it is extremely educational,' and he described a lovely occasion when he'd been asked to go and talk to the 'War and Society' summer school at the Open University and he sat next to a woman who turned out to have developed her first interest in history from watching *The World at War* and she'd gone on to enrol in the Open University and here she was on a second level course.

Then at one point over dinner when we knew that he was going to get the Channel 4 job and we were congratulating him, he sat there and said, 'But we've got this amazing responsibility to do all of this educational programming and I have no idea what to do about it.' Of course, to have a Channel with 15 per cent of the output mandated to education was extraordinary. And I cheerfully banged the table and said, 'I know exactly what you should do about it,' and proceeded to talk about what could be done. We went on with this conversation and towards the end of the dinner he sort of looked at me and said, 'If I was to advertise a job that looked like this…how likely would you be to apply for it?' Prickles went up the back of my neck and I suddenly thought he could be serious. A few days later the phone rang and it was Jeremy. He said that he'd gone 'nap' on getting me appointed without interview, but that they wanted to interview me, and I sort of gasped, because I hadn't taken him that seriously, and I had to phone him back that night and say if I was going to be serious. Clearly, you wouldn't turn down a chance like that, even though it was a bit frightening, and later on I went and got interviewed by Anne Sofer and Edmund Dell in the way he describes in his book.[1]

Catterall: So you had a clear vision of what you wanted to do with this 15 per cent of the Channel?

Sargant: Well, I knew it had to be done differently from the basic educational programming on the other channels, because to fill 15 per cent we had to cast it more broadly.

Catterall: You did believe strongly that television can be an effective means of education?

Sargant: Well, we already had at the higher level the Open University on the BBC, which had opened up opportunities as well as providing knowledge for people. At the other end we'd already had adult literacy programmes triggering lots of responses, and more recently I had been running the evaluation of a numeracy project which had been done by Yorkshire Television. We knew the power of all of this.

When I was appointed (as a two-year temporary research officer at the Open University) my very first task was to research into Access (then called Gateway) courses. They were done by the BBC and the National Extension College to encourage people to think about studying, perhaps with the Open University. So there was a maths course, 'Square Two', social psychology, 'Man in Society', and a radio course, 'Reading to Learn'. They reached very large numbers of people and I did the first monitoring of all that. They were accompanied by textbooks and by classes up and down the country. So I knew that there were more things to be done at the higher education level than the Open University could do.

Catterall: So you had a vision of education for different age groups and levels?

Sargant: Yes. I was chairing the National Gas Consumers Council and serving on the National Consumer Council and the notion of consumer education, of adults having better information and being able to make better decisions about their lives and being stimulated into a wider variety of activities – that was all in my head. We had a more precise thing we wanted to do as well, though it wasn't the main thing at that stage, which was to offer some lower level analogue for the Open University, to do something like an Open College which might reach the people who left school at 16.

I'd been doing national planning for continuing education, but that wasn't saying it would all be at the higher education level. We were saying we needed a range of levels where people could come in and out. And one of the interesting things was to think about an outcome which was simply that somebody's imagination was stimulated. What it wasn't conceived as was formal, sequential, curriculum-led education in the way that educational broadcasting had heretofore basically been thought of. A brilliant thing about the freedom Jeremy gave me was that, in agreeing there were a number of goals like reaching the unemployed, like consumer education, like political education (which I conceived of as active democracy), the *In Sickness and in Health* strand and the programming for the over-60s, there were

The Educational Output

a number of areas where you didn't need to treat it as a piece of curriculum.

What both Jeremy and I were deeply committed to was the idea of television as a very powerful medium for reaching older people. What we did for them was a magazine format in which you could mix entertainment, informative items and things you could follow up. And the consumer show as well essentially had a strong educational agenda on advice, information and consumer issues. And we put that out at 8.30pm for everyone. And the heavy duty stuff had a slot regularly at 6.30pm, which had never been committed by any channel before, for basic skills like literacy and numeracy. So what we were doing was complementing some of this more open material with the heavy duty stuff.

Catterall: The 15 per cent. Was there a clear commitment to schedule this across the Channel rather than in particular slots?

Sargant: What happened was that Jeremy did a basic schedule and said to all of us in principle that we could count on these sorts of slots. Education had quite a lot of them, so in a sense everyone else was a bit jealous of us. In another sense we were a bit fed up because it was felt that he was being a bit labelling. At the beginning we had a sequence of 5.30pm slots, and then we had a sequence of 6.30pm slots. Since we then only went on air at 5.30pm the 5.30pm slots were technically the pits for the Channel, but for anyone else they would have been considered pretty good slots, particularly for those up North where it is already teatime. So we had about eight of these 5.30pm and 6.30pm slots, and then we had a prize of an 8.30pm on Tuesdays and a 10.00pm on a Friday, which we immediately identified as the medical/health one, because we knew that we needed a late night slot to take on some of those issues. Then we had a Saturday lunchtime slot. That was our basic schedule. So we needed to choose what to put in the 5.30pm slots. We started off with one of the over-60s programmes there. We had one of the physical fitness programmes of my colleague Carol Haslam there as well, and my unemployed strand because the unemployed were at home more during the day. Then into the 6.30pm slots we put the basic skills, the classic arts and things such as geology....

Catterall: Science?

Sargant: No. In my needs mapping I had science and technology and another one called 'ways of seeing', which was a bundle of things visual, which were not allocated against these slots. There was an editorial decision that we would not have a regular science and technology programme coming out of education because it was to be given as a special agenda, along with the arts, to *Channel 4 News*. These were fundamental early editorial decisions. We later got health and medicine out of current affairs. The bundle that Liz [Forgan] had was so overwhelming that some of these areas, like the difficult negotiations with IBT, descended to us, so I became the picker-up of some of the unconsidered trifles.

With 'Ways of Seeing' I argued with Jeremy that it was a visual medium and that the country was profoundly under-educated in things visual, and that I wanted to integrate photography, art, design and all things visual in a different way. And when he did our first allocation of slots and money, and accepted some priorities and rejected others, I argued for 'Ways of Seeing' with him. He went off and came back next morning and said he really liked the idea and he had changed his budgets around and found an extra £1.2 million for me. And he said I didn't have to commission in the standard series based way, with half an hour slots (the medical/health one was three quarters of an hour), but I could use the £1.2 million for anything which fitted the 'Ways of Seeing' criteria, commission them, and he would schedule them when he saw what they looked like. So that was for me the most exciting thing because it took me into Tom Keating,[2] it took me into *Pottery Ladies*, it took me into Tudor miniatures, it took me into a whole range of wonderful visual arts programmes which were really exciting and which ultimately caused me to be made a Honorary Fellow of the Royal College of Art, because Chris Frayling[3] said I'd done so much for accessible arts programming.

Catterall: Was the 15 per cent always a boon, or could it be a straitjacket?

Sargant: I think it was very much resented and worried about, because there had never been a commitment of that kind. The person who didn't worry was Jeremy. If you go back to my appointment I think

The Educational Output

there were large numbers of people who would have given their back teeth for my job. I was of course dead scared of it and I went to the person who would be my opposite number at the BBC, a man called Don Grattan, whom I knew very well through the Open University, and one Friday evening I asked him about the idea that I might go for that job. He said, 'What a brilliant idea. If you don't go for it tell me and I'll go for it instead.' So it was a deeply coveted position. But the honour ought to go to Jeremy who was completely idealistic and brilliant about it. He gave me, as he said, not the best but very decent budgets, and the best of all is that he didn't tell me in any way that it had to be in any particular televisual form. The limits were my own imagination. He actually only ever turned down one particular proposition, about wine. It was an extraordinary time.

Catterall: And you never had any trouble in filling the 15 per cent?

Sargant: No. What I was trying to do was directly commission about five and a half hours a week of things which were initiated by me or by Carol, and afterwards by our assistant editor. They could range from gardening to adult literacy. Then we were adding to that an average of about two hours each week, so there was no way we could be got at by the IBA, which we took from documentary series, which we wrapped around and provided run-up and follow-up material, for instance, you made an educational happening around arts broadcasts, with programme notes and a documentary. We started off many of these strategies which are now pretty well taken for granted both on Channel 4 and BBC2. One example was an arts broadcast such as the National Theatre's production of *The Oresteia*. We also started off seasons, the first big example of that being the Peter Montagnon series, *The Heart of the Dragon*, about China. There was a book and a study guide and all the rest of it.

This was the justification for Carol's dual remit, because she was bringing in the documentary series that were to form quite a lot of this output. She was also doing it with a genuine educational background, so she was extremely good and caring about it all. She did a lot of the wildlife stuff and got into not just the medical and health but also the environment and development stuff.

Catterall: Did you have her as a colleague because of the size of your brief?

Sargant: At that early stage it wasn't common. Jeremy appointed the three key senior commissioning editors, myself, Liz Forgan and David Rose. That caused the flak because two of us were women, which was of course unheard of at that time, and two of us were not even out of television, which was also unheard of. There was this charming speech by Gus McDonald[4] at the Edinburgh Television Festival in which he used this wonderful word, 'underwhelmed' regarding our appointments. We were not treated with great courtesy. Mike Scott[5] and the rest at Granada refused to deal with Liz and me in the early days. They all wanted to deal with Jeremy. I had the task of dealing with children's programming, as well as educational programming, as well as audience research. So I had to go through an IBA children's consultation about what we would do at the beginning. The rest of them couldn't believe that I was representing this Channel when I knew zilch. The ITV people really thought that they were going to own us and run us and command us much more than turned out.

The IBA also thought they had some sort of parental ownership, particularly in the educational area. They had a great big advisory council and they were going to vet what we did. The first thing I had to do was produce elaborate proposals for all the series which they had to approve for a whole year in advance, before I could even do any commissioning. It would never have got on air! Only later did I discover that they had expected me to go and ask them to help and advise me.

There was also an IBA co-ordinating committee with the ITV companies, and the IBA had required the ITV companies to appoint community liaison officers. The assumption was that they would form a unit, run by the IBA, to do the back-up to all of our programmes. That did not happen and was not acceptable. It partly did not happen because we were commissioning a lot of independents. I can remember catching a taxi with David Plowright,[6] and he said he wasn't going to spend a penny of his liaison officer's money backing up a programme made by an independent.

I took advice from people like Don Grattan, Controller of Education at the BBC. As a result, I went off to the agency, Broadcasting Support Services, which had originally been set up to support adult literacy, and talked with them about educational follow-up, contracting with them to do it. We were very material in them building up to the size they are now. Essentially I decided, having

The Educational Output

taken advice, to throw our lot in with them rather than try to set up a separate organisation. Presumably I intuitively wasn't happy with the idea of it being done by the regulator, the IBA.

Catterall: Did the IBA ever come back to you about the educational content?

Sargant: Oh yes. They had an Education Advisory Council with very posh people on it. They had Geoffrey Holland from the Manpower Services Commission, Peter Newsam from the Inner London Education Authority and so on. The guy who was scrutinising my first set of proposals was Sir William Taylor.[7] I remember that vividly, because he was looking quizzically at headings like 'for people with more time than money', and I said to him, 'If I had called these strands for the unemployed or consumer education and so on you wouldn't be arguing with me now.' He said, 'No, I suppose not.' It was an attempt to change the image. If we were to have such a large chunk of the Channel devoted to education it couldn't be presented as education in a formal way. That would have been death for the Channel. So I had to find a way of opening it up and presenting it. The key thing was that Jeremy, in giving us good slots, had been honourable about the handicapped, the over-60s and so on. Showing the IBA that we had these good slots and proper goals meant that the IBA in turn agreed to extend their definition of education to include basic skills, cookery or gardening. We had some of the most serious gardening programmes, for example, about seeds and propagation, *Plants for Free*, which got 4.3 million viewers on Friday evenings at 9pm, much to the chagrin of the entertainment commissioning editors on the Channel. It was the trick of at the same time facing the IBA with your conscience and facing the audience with life-enhancing stuff which worked. Much of this has now become the model for the current infotainment programmes, and my work was really the beginning of that.

Catterall: And where did the 15 per cent come from?

Sargant: It wasn't statutory. The statutory bit was that there should be a given proportion of programmes of an educational nature. The IBA turned that into 15 per cent, which at that time meant about an hour a day [at that time].

Jeremy understood the importance of all of this, and we made an early appointment of Derek Jones as Education Liaison Officer. He did this very well, and Jeremy also made available a very decent budget of £250,000 for us to do that back-up and educational support.

Initially there was this tiny corpus of people. The three senior commissioning editors, Liz Forgan, David Rose and me, arrived on 1 April 1981 and were there with Paul Bonner, Jeremy, John Ranelagh, Justin Dukes and Ellis Griffiths. Then Jeremy put out the advert that got the 6,000 responses, and it is from these people that the next tranche of commissioning editors were to come. And over those summer months we were getting a sense of the workload and the quantity of proposals, and we had no model at all of how to handle them. Liz had all the news *and* factual programmes, so she was alarmingly overwhelmed. That is how we moved to the notion of relieving some part of my and Liz's work using one of the next tranche of commissioning editors, and that is how the documentary series and the wildlife stuff got carved off from Liz, the medical/health stuff got moved over into education, and half of Carol's time, as one of the new commissioning editors, was to be allocated to education and half to documentary series directly under Jeremy.

Catterall: How did you go about commissioning?

Sargant: We were getting presented with very large numbers of ideas.[8] I then went into formally listing everything against a dozen topics, and started to talk to those that looked intuitively as though they fitted in. I took the view that we were to be a Channel to publish other people's ideas, we were designed to be innovative, we were not supposed to be following our own proclivities. In that sense I think I differed from some of the others. Because I was not a producer myself I wasn't coming at it with ten of my own ideas. I was standing back. Over the years we put on things like beekeeping and *Mushroom Magic*, quirky ideas that hadn't been thought about before. If there was a brilliant idea which I thought fitted in with people's lives and had an educational intent and outcome – it didn't have to have an educational format – then fine. My test was 'What happens if it works', and programme makers had to tell me whether their idea was likely to trigger somebody to want to go to an art gallery or something.

There was an interesting issue which I think I had to deal with

The Educational Output

more than the others. Most of the ITV people wanted to make programmes for Channel 4. They saw it as an extra way of using their production facilities, and they offered packages of programmes. Jeremy wanted to work collegially, they were going to be selling our airtime. Having more airtime than most of my colleagues, some of whom were very cynical about the ITV companies, I paid more attention to ensuring that I had at least one commission from each of the ITV companies. I landed up with some visual art programming from LWT plus a long series of history lectures. Granada was interesting. Mike Scott was a belated gardener, but he'd never been able to get a decent slot on ITV, and I could offer him a 6.30pm slot on Thursdays. He put on it a guy who had worked at the Open University and then for the broadcaster and naturalist David Attenborough, and a guy who had worked in adult education making astonishingly good gardening programmes, beautifully shot and directed, made for me by Granada out of a local programme budget. So there was an element of choosing what I wanted but negotiating to get the best value.

Yorkshire Television had been making solid educational programmes for ITV for some time. We made the serious forerunner of the Open College programmes with them, called *Making Sense of Economics*, in which Zeinab Bedawi became a national figure. We went on to *Making Sense of Marketing*. They had been doing the numeracy stuff and so I commissioned them to update that and make a new series. So we made a major commitment of three ten part series on numeracy and kept on running it in the 6.30pm slot. Jeremy was meanwhile prepared to do something no-one else had done, which was repeat educational programmes if they were good enough. All of this helped me make my money go round. If I got deals with ITV which were quite cheap then I could spend more money on the independents, who didn't have the same resources behind them.

Catterall: Did you have a problem getting the ITV companies to see what your vision was?

Sargant: Well, I think probably at the first meeting, but not thereafter. Once they had met us more than once they realised we were serious people. The interesting thing about ITV was that I had been head of the Marketing Department at Enfield, now Middlesex University. So I had been teaching marketing, and this was a time when people were beginning to understand about segmented and differentiated marketing. Now I always knew with Channel 4 that we were talking to national specialist audiences and not to mass regional audiences. But the ITV companies were used to this mass regional marketing and this is what all their structures were about.

Catterall: Which presumably had implications for how they sold your airtime?

Sargant: Exactly. What I argued from quite early on was that our space needed to be sold separately. That was outwith their structures, understandably, because their imperatives were to increase the size of the regional advertising cake that they owned. Nobody in their system had had an imperative to increase the size of the whole ITV cake. So basically they adopted a strategy of selling our time as clamp-on ITV time, and not as having a national specialist character. The interesting thing is that the audience researchers at the BBC knew exactly the national specialist story and knew that our research needs were coterminous with theirs,[9] and not with ITV's. But my initial attempts to have the new BARB research arrangements allow for decent national specialist demographics, for example, to sell against gardening or whatever were completely vitiated.

Catterall: So you had no idea of the size of your potential advertising audience?

Sargant: It actually had a more direct impact than that. Take, for instance, *Years Ahead*, the over-60s show, which built up to over 2 million viewers at 3.45 in the afternoon, which at that time in Channel 4 was quite something. Not only was there a denial that older people have any money, which is ludicrous. But think about Thames Television, for instance, selling our advertising as clamp-on space. This meant that we would have a programme for the over-60s, whilst around it you would have completely inappropriate advertising. This went on all the time. Even when we had the Open College going out at lunchtime you would have completely inappropriate advertising sold by ITV. They simply sold clamp-on space. They didn't think. My joke was always to use Damart thermal underwear as an example of what you might advertise instead. And *Years Ahead* had a three-

The Educational Output

quarters of an hour slot, which would have been allowed to have a centre advertising break by the IBA, but for the whole of the eight years it ran the ITV companies never exercised their right to open up an advertising break in the middle of that programme. They never even sold any gardening advertising, even though the gardening programme was getting bigger audiences than the BBC equivalent. It was very unimaginative of them and it would have been perfectly feasible and rational for them to have peeled off a specialist national sales force to focus on selling Channel 4 specialist space, exactly as Channel 4 now does. They could have negotiated a way to carve up the commission between them. But they would never do it, so it was always clear to me that as soon as Channel 4 was allowed to sell its own advertising space it would clean up. But that wasn't even evident to most of our own bosses.

I most vividly remember a dinner with the ITV Board, with Jill McIvor[10] in particular, at which I argued the folly of not selling space separately, and she formally told me off. It was astonishing that they were so ignorant about what was actually marketing common sense.

There never had been space for gardening or arts and culture programmes on ITV, because of the need for mass audiences. But TVS made a lovely series for us with Jonathan Miller in which he went through the staging of *Fidelio*, and Edwin Mullins did a wonderful programme about different artists' interpretations of Paradise. So one was able to offer even the most 'boring' ITV companies like TVS the possibility of really creative programming that they wouldn't have got on ITV, and to which they really responded.

Another nice thing, thinking of my social science background, was setting up with Thames, *Citizen 2000*, in which we selected 20 children who were born in 1982, who would therefore become citizens in 2000, and they have been followed systematically since. That has been a very ambitious and thoughtful piece of observation. I know that Granada has done the *Seven Up* series which has now been taken over by the BBC, but we've followed them every year, not just every seven years. So I think with a bit of care and thought one was able to turn these relationships with ITV companies, which might have been difficult, to good advantage.

Catterall: Presumably Jeremy didn't agree with you on the selling of advertising?

Sargant: No, it wasn't that at all. Jeremy wasn't into that sort of thing. He was the classic creative programme maker. I remember vividly walking across Hyde Park with him from a finance meeting, trying to tell him about the nature of the audience, when people got home from work and when we should be scheduling for what sort of people. He wasn't against it, it just wasn't how his mind worked.

If the Labour party had won the 1979 election they would have legislated for an Open Broadcasting Foundation with commissioning. Given that they lost the election, you then have this extraordinary British compromise of virtually all of these ideals, except for the public funding. That was a political decision, that was not for Jeremy to decide. But because the remit set up in the Act is so generous, the distinctive programming, the 'catering for tastes not otherwise catered for', one didn't have to worry about the money. You didn't want anything the ITV companies were doing in selling the space to mess you up, and you ruefully thought that they could make more money out of us if they were more intelligent about marketing, but it wasn't up to any of us to rock that boat, nor was there any point. So I don't think this would have become top of Jeremy's agenda for quite a long time.

Of course, by the 1988 White Paper and the build-up to the 1990 Broadcasting Act there was quite a different flavour to the government, and the threat by that point was privatisation. The worry was that Michael Grade[11] would not stand up against it, and Michael was forgiven a lot by Liz because he stood up against privatisation.

Catterall: Getting back to educational programming, did an enormous number of ideas emerge from independents at the start?

Sargant: There were an enormous number of ideas, many from new companies. For example, *Years Ahead* came in from a small group in Scotland. The producers had got interested in the over-60s from making stuff for the Scottish Health Education Council about confusion in the elderly. This completely new little company called Skyline came in with a proposal called 'Vistas', but they wanted to do what we wanted to do. I started engaging with them about how it might come out, and no-one else was putting in an over-60s programme that was any better, so we went with it. We finally called it *Years Ahead* rather than Vistas because, well, Tom Keating said to me, 'If you are my age, you know, there is only one vista and that's down.'

The Educational Output

Some of them were even more idealistic than that. We had a woman who was just a housewife with a mentally handicapped child, who wanted to do programming for mentally handicapped children. One of my strands was children with special needs (because when I went to that ITV consultation they were doing all the mainline children's stuff, but no-one was doing anything in that special needs category).

Jeremy did have a number of mates who were very good programme makers, and so he would occasionally get me to see somebody who I knew he really cared about. Normally I agreed with him and would try to find space. At the very beginning there was a group of programmes from Susanna Capon. She wanted to make multicultural programmes for children, which was exactly in our remit. Related to that was this woman who wanted to make programmes for mentally handicapped children. She had got the children's writer David Wood to work with her. She got the idea of setting the series in the office of a children's comic, with a dog who was dumb and a comic made which would be attached to it. She didn't have a programme maker so I put out some feelers and we located some very good children's programme makers, and they made this lovely series called *Chip's Comic*. It had a black girl editor, all very PC, but it was brilliantly done with a medic who specialised in mental handicap working with it to set the learning agenda. So I went into some unorthodox things because nobody told me I couldn't.

Some of the things came down the line from people like Michael Kustow.[12] The *Tom Keating on Painters* series came into him, and of course it wasn't arts in Michael's sense of the word. But Tom was an absolutely mesmerising guy and what he was doing in each programme was showing how to create a Turner or a Rembrandt. It wasn't high art, but it was brilliant for making people think about how a painting is created and encouraging them to paint. The letters that came in on lined writing paper, you know the English thing with lined writing paper... And this series came from two young men who just set up a company and wrote in with half a dozen ideas. So it was extremely exciting, all these people setting up companies in order to make programmes they were passionate about, and because they were passionate the programmes breathed.

Catterall: But there were passionate programmes that were seen as a bit of a problem, like IBT.

The Making of Channel 4

Sargant: Some of the programmes which had a social agenda behind the information required much greater care about the tone of voice. IBT was a group of incredibly caring different organisations dealing with development education. They been waiting for something like Channel 4 to arrive to stimulate their outreach with all of their little local groups. They touched on tough agendas, such as the relationship between rich and poor nations. There was a very political series which came out of the same genre, Jeremy Seabrook talking about poverty. You've got people coming from different political perspectives and they were harsh and there were quite a few of those. IBT was part of our educational output. They'd asked for dozens of series, flooding Liz, and it was quite clear that they were educational and that they shouldn't be dealt with by Liz. I had more experience, coming from my background, of dealing with these sorts of idealistic groups. I discussed this with them knowing that we couldn't possibly commission them to do the amazing amount they asked for and finally guaranteed them something like two series, to my shame and to Jeremy's slight annoyance, because their pressure was aggravating us all. I knew we had to give them something. Jeremy sent me a note the next day saying, 'That's okay, I wish you'd talked to me about it before you sent the letter though.'

We didn't yet know at that stage what this assorted group of people were going to want. That's because, unusually, they were asking for this collaboration on programmes to reach out to their network of discussion groups. They were not a production company, and only when we gave them the commission could they put together a production team. At that point I handed it over to my colleague Carol Haslam, who had just joined the Channel. I wasn't party to the discussion of the content.

However, IBT is still going, still involved with broadcasters, still making programmes. Its cause is the education of the public about Third World and development issues, and we're now some 15 years later. It is still extremely worthwhile. If in the beginning two or three years there were one or two programmes that were slightly grating or harsh voices, then I think it got out of proportion. It didn't get very good audiences because it was quite hard viewing. But we were charged with having these other voices. We didn't just want bland documentaries, we did want something working with all these educational groups. I cannot remember which series it was which

The Educational Output

really upset Edmund [Dell], but it is odd that this became one of the things which really worried him when it was just one out of 50 or 60 educational commissions. If I'd been at the Board I probably could have dealt with it. But IBT did several series. One was about Third World debt, but there were a number of others which we classified as political education. It was a brave attempt to put it on the screen in a way which hadn't been done before. I don't think we did it brilliantly, but I don't think it's something we should be ashamed of.

Catterall: Was part of the problem the issue of balance?

Sargant: I'm sure it was reflected in some of the political education coverage. It wasn't political education in the Ruskin sense, but it was about voting and such issues. I'm sure at that time we had people who had these frustrated voices and some of it was grating. Carol Haslam, who worked with them, would have thought that it was balanced enough and probably for someone like her, very keen on development issues, it was. But I think what was different for us, as opposed to current affairs, was that week on week we were putting out varieties of programmes. There wasn't necessarily balance within a series, but there was a varied diet across the output. The odd development series didn't seem to upset this balance.

What we did try to change more of was that we were mainly getting men's views of the world. I vividly remember two examples. There was a proposed series about innovation in education, and all the six innovators were male. No mention of Margaret Macmillan, Maria Montessori, etc. Similarly there was a medical/health series proposal which didn't have a single programme in about women's issues.

We all came up with our own operating principles. One of mine was not to put my own prejudices on proposals, because I was there as an enabler and as a publisher. But if something did come in with only male voices and male topics, both Carol and I would discuss it with them and ask them to cover the ground better. Sometimes they were happy with that and went away and did, and other times they didn't.

A precise example was a proposal called 'The Blood of the British'. I was fascinated by the idea of doing something to complement Sue Woodford's multicultural remit. So I was prepared to commission a series about 'race'. I had one series made by TVS called *Passage to*

Britain about contemporary waves of immigration. Then there was this archaeological proposal, 'The Blood of the British', dealing with earlier waves of immigration! However, its author was an old-fashioned programme maker who had been at the BBC, and he wanted to do it with John Julius Norwich. I had never seen John Julius Norwich but I knew he was one of the standard BBC faces, and one of the facets of BBC presentations was that they had presenters who hadn't been intimately involved in the text. I went so far as to go to a viewing room in Soho to see if John Julius Norwich would fit. He really wouldn't. So I went back to them and said that I really liked the idea but was it possible to find another presenter, preferably a bright, young, lively woman. They went off and found a wonderful archaeologist from Newnham [College, Cambridge] called Catherine Hills. It taught me two things. Firstly, that you could do this. Secondly, we put the series on after 11pm with variable time slots and it still got over 1 million viewers. This was quite early on in the Channel's history. And because she was herself an archaeologist she got a level of response on the digs she went to that no standard presenter would have got. One of the things I pushed after that was using an expert to present who could therefore give their own input. You got a much livelier and more intelligent level of educational programming than we had heretofore been used to. I did try to bring in good women presenters: Jancis Robinson, Heather Couper, Carol Vorderman, Zeinab Badawi, Floella Benjamin and Ruth Pitt all fronted education programmes. At one point I even had three heavily pregnant presenters, Penny Junor, Jancis Robinson and Floella Benjamin, and nobody had ever put heavily pregnant women on screen before. That really did start to change things.

And I had strong women programme makers who had been marginalised. The television world was full of men. Channel 4 was the first time that any channel had a large number of women commissioning, and by the middle of it half of our management committee was women. And I had more women than men programme makers, so I don't think they needed to make programmes specifically about women.

Catterall: We've talked about IBT, can you tell me anything about the Greek Civil War programme?

The Educational Output

Sargant: That was a commission of Carol Haslam's in her documentary series role, so I wouldn't know a great deal about it, except that at the end of it many felt that the series had been manipulated by the young woman producer who had presented part of the story and not the other side. I remember sitting at dinner with Sir Nicholas Henderson[13] and his wife, who was Greek, at the time it was being transmitted, and they were horribly upset by it, but I think it caught all of us unawares.

Catterall: Does it raise the problem of how you present these narratives using a very powerful medium?

Sargant: I think that the serious issue is that people who are given the task of commissioning have the very heavy task of trying to ensure the proposals they have are solidly rooted in evidence. If one is given a proposal about a politically tendentious area it is important to judge it. That Greek series definitely represented a partial view. It was one, relatively small documentary series, but it was a partial view. I don't think there were many of those. There was a sensitivity about balance, not within a programme but across a swathe of programmes. If you are dealing with lots of independents, the idea of balancing inside each programme or each series is much more difficult, but across the whole piece it should be possible.

The problem at the beginning was that all us commissioning editors were putting in similar topics, almost by accident. At one point virtually every factual series, whether it was education, youth, religion or current affairs, included the women camped at Greenham Common, even my over-60s show. When we discovered this we agreed that Liz would run a sort of co-ordinating committee, so we all once a fortnight or so shared with her the topics we might be covering over the next couple of months, in case everyone was going to go down and film Greenham Common or whatever again, in order to avoid ridiculous clashes.

Catterall: So you'd re-schedule things?

Sargant: Or if it was a magazine programme made every week we'd simply ask them not to do that item that week because at least two others are doing it as well. Don't go to Sizewell B [nuclear power station], somebody else has just been there. We could do that collegially, without that being censorship, simply common sense. That mechanism worked quite well in the early days, before it became more structured.

Catterall: But there was a lot of press criticism initially.

Sargant: Undoubtedly some of the programmes were less than well made. There were new programme makers, Alan Fountain[14] had a lot of independent workshops making quite innovatory stuff. But they seemed to me to get protected from a lot of the criticism because they were labelled as workshops and put out late at night. It was difficult at the beginning. We went off to this retreat with the journalists hanging around to see if heads would roll, and Jeremy was being very sensible about it. We knew that we had already done 17 months commissioning, and that all this stuff was already coming through and that such changes as we might make would therefore be more in the scheduling and the presentation. So we didn't actually change what we were doing at that point, but the public perception started to change.

It is true that at the beginning the screen looked a bit stupid because of the IPA-Equity strike. But I always thought, firstly that people did soon get a bit used to the idea and secondly that the kerfuffle over TV-AM made our performance look good by comparison. It was the first time that a whole new channel had come on air in that short a time period and we got on air successfully, with very decent programming.

Our style of commissioning changed into 1984. One of the interesting things is that ITV had run series of 13 or 26 parts, and people were in the habit of making really large chunks of programming. At the very beginning we had to fill an incredible quantity of space because we hadn't started to build up our own library of repeats. There was acres of space. I remember a wonderful story about Jeremy waking up having nightmares about a blank screen. I managed to fill my remit by also taking some of the best of the available repeats from ITV. Some people could do that more than others. And Jeremy knew quite a lot about the quality of other people's programmes, and of good things which had never got a repeat before. So he did some clever American buying, which Michael Grade obviously went on with afterwards, but he also did some very clever repeats. But we did them usually with some sort of innovation. For

The Educational Output

example, he decided to give a second run to his own *The World at War*, but what he did was to get me to commission four three-quarter hour programmes updating it, bringing in new evidence and having people discuss it. So we turned to good account the fact that we were repeating it.

At the very beginning we had these long runs,[15] but we were getting all these proposals from independents and we didn't have any flexibility to fit them in given all these 13-week blocks. So by the time we got to our second commissioning round the pattern was changed.

Catterall: And the commissioning round covered what time period?

Sargant: Well, at the beginning we planned 17 months, and a lot of stuff was bought in and we had a whole queue of stuff waiting to be broadcast because everybody had got over-anxious to start off with. At that point there was a more serious look at how to present and schedule the material. By then we were being more sensible about the most naff programmes and we were much more sensitive about presentation and scheduling. I don't think it took a long time to sort out. We then learned the ways to win brownie points. For example, here was I having a consumer show on Tuesday evenings, but I'd also taken in the first of three series called *Take Six Cooks*. At that point cookery programmes were seen as afternoon programmes for housewives. Now Thames had a really good stable of people, I think it's no accident that Jeremy had been Director of Programmes there before. And they had made the first of these upmarket cookery programmes, with Kay Avila going into the kitchens of some of our best contemporary chefs. It was really intelligent and well done and we put it out at an 8.30pm slot, and that was the breakthrough. That was also at the time of year when the other channels were playing repeats, in the summer. So we learned that if we put our good new programmes out in the summer we got much better coverage. I remember vividly when my first wine programme with Jancis Robinson went out in the summer and it was brilliantly received. So I think we got cleverer and more thoughtful.

The second thing we did was stop commissioning in these 13 week chunks. We started commissioning more in six parts and in my area sometimes in ten parts for more systematic education series such as economics and marketing. If I had to get through a year with a serious slot and I was also trying to be sensible with money I would have three ten-part series and then fill in the holiday breaks with shorter, livelier series. I think we just got a bit more experienced. I don't think initially Jeremy was thinking like that, he was thinking about individual programmes, not about how the Channel became more than the sum of its parts. Nor, I think, was Paul [Bonner]. We had very good presentation, but we weren't considering how to place all the stuff within it to its best advantage.

Catterall: You, because of your background, were clearly conscious of the audience, but the mix of programmes at the start seemed calculated to destroy an audience.

Sargant: That's true. The evidence was that we weren't getting an inheritance factor from one programme to the next. We had minority audiences and that inheritance factor which had been the basis of all Andrew Ehrenberg's audience research,[16] the proportion who would stay to watch the next programme, on which the whole of the strategy about audiences had been constructed, simply didn't work for us. Just getting people to know there was another choice and to use the fourth button was the first big behavioural change one had to encourage.

The one area that was looked at was the Friday night audience, because the light entertainment people were very keen on the idea of Friday night. The BBC had always had its gardening programme on Fridays and we moved our gardening programme to Fridays and we started to get evidence of people crossing from BBC1 to watch our gardening programme and the light entertainment people didn't like it one bit because in the middle of their programmes, often with smaller audiences, was this whopping audience for a gardening programme.

After the appointment of Sue Stoessl a year or so in, formally to be in charge of marketing, I obviously didn't continue to have anything to do with the marketing brief I'd had in the early days. I did, in a sense, intellectually, fall out with her. She came from LWT and seemed to me to import all the attitudes to our audience measurement that ITV had had, when I had spent the first year trying to build up awareness of national specialist audiences. But what she did do which was very valuable for education was to commission large sample surveys of the population as a whole, asking them about their reactions to the series they had watched and the educational follow-up and back-up. For the IBA each year I produced a report demonstrating what we had done in

The Educational Output

educational programming, what the strands were, what the audiences were, what the back-up was, whether the audience had followed the series up. We included quite a lot of the other factual series as well and provided analyses of the composition of the audience, whether we were reaching the less well-educated and so on. So Sue was extremely helpful in constructing that, because the BARB stuff couldn't tell me what I needed to know for it. This then caused my commissioning editor colleagues to ask why she couldn't study their series as well, so we gradually extended it. We could then factor this information into future commissioning and demonstrate to the IBA that we were fulfilling our remit.

My original profession had been market research. I had spent 12 years at the Gallup Poll, so audience research was familiar territory to me. At the beginning when I was doing the Channel 4 audience research I sat there with the ITV guys and talked about how they presented the data. I demanded from them that they did the percentage of our audience against the current reach of the Channel, rather than against the whole population, given that our transmissions didn't reach everyone at the start. They wouldn't concede this, saying it wasn't necessary. I told them that when the audience share of the Channel went up from three to four per cent it would be front page news, and indeed it was. In contrast, when Channel 5 was launched as the fifth terrestrial channel in 1997, they similarly demanded that their audience figures should be percentaged on their lesser reach, because they cannot reach the whole population, and this was agreed. When we set off we could only reach 75 per cent of the population, and yet this wasn't agreed. But at the start we almost certainly did have four per cent of the people we could actually reach.

The interesting thing for me was that, because we had so much minority programming, whereas on other channels my educational stuff would have been at the narrow cast end, on Channel 4 my material was solidly in the middle in terms of audience appeal. Drama was more popular, but I was getting higher audiences for many of my programmes than much of the rest of the Channel. I got 1.5 million at 11pm for three one-hour observational documentaries of three mentally handicapped people going to live in the community, and 2 million for *Years Ahead* at 3.45pm was good. In contrast it took quite a long time to get the current affairs documentaries like *Cutting Edge* up to decent audiences. But the area which never gets high audiences, and

I used to feel bad about it, was arts and culture, no matter what it was. So some of this lovely visual stuff I was doing, even though it got amazingly high reaction ratings, would never tip over the million mark. But I think that says more about this country than it does about Channel 4. Even *Mushroom Magic* got over 2 million on a Friday evening.

Catterall: The audience profiles weren't broken down into gender and ethnic background, etc?

Sargant: There are two things, the ratings and the appreciation indices. It is often the case that a low audience has a very high appreciation. In the special surveys I could always separate men and women. You couldn't really separate out ethnicity. The samples were never big enough to give a meaningful number.

Catterall: How much freedom did you have in programming?

Sargant: Complete. Quite extraordinary. It's absolutely true that one went to Jeremy and said, I want to commission this, this and this. He didn't put any boundaries on me. Once I knew my programme judgement was alright I stopped worrying. I would present a coherent set of proposals against a number of goals which we had agreed, within a budget framework which I had been allowed.

Catterall: Did you have to negotiate the budget?

Sargant: At the beginning he gave it to us, and after that we went on negotiating it. The main thing at the beginning was cutting everybody down to allow for the fact that we needed to start to use our own repeats and we wanted to put the money into new programmes.

I tried to insist on not just having education in predictable slots, but on doing what I called 'happiness' programmes, beekeeping or whatever. Liz Forgan couldn't stand the idea, and neither could Mike Bolland,[17] of doing a six-part series about mushrooms, they thought that was really ridiculous. But I also wanted something about imagination, and what will touch people's hearts and minds. So I went back in year five and, because they'd made such a fuss about patchwork when we'd shown it right at the start of the Channel, I

The Educational Output

insisted on repeating *Quilts in Women's Lives* and commissioning a new series on patchwork. Jeremy allowed me to do all of these things.

The head of film and television at the Arts Council, Rodney Wilson, suggested a one-hour programme on the women who had become pottery makers, called *Pottery Ladies*. It was brilliant and the material was stunning. It was so rich that we were able to make a four-part series out of it. Nobody said to me, you can't do that. So we had this series which showed the women's lives, their craft, how they painted and the rest of it. Otherwise it would have been a sterile, one-hour, standard Arts Council documentary.

There was a wonderful animator, Lesley Keen, up in Glasgow. She brought in a fantastic story board to me at the very beginning about Paul Klee. She wanted to animate his art, calling it *Taking a Line for a Walk*. It became the most astonishing 12-minute animation. We then formed the idea of doing a half an hour documentary about how one creates such a piece of animation with her. This was quite early on. We transmitted this in an hour slot, the animation, then the documentary and then the animation again, because it was very dense and visually exciting. Jeremy sent me a note the next day saying that this was one of the best things the Channel had ever done. The point is that he let me do it, at 8pm on a Thursday night.

She did another one later on, using visually a Grecian vase motif. We did the same sort of trick, she did a six-minute animation of the story of Orpheus and Eurydice, and then we did a documentary in the middle on the various interpretations of the story, in opera, drama, film, etc, and then we showed the animation again. She won the Scottish equivalent of a BAFTA for that.

So Jeremy didn't slot me as any other television boss would have done, and I don't remember him ever saying no or complaining, except when it took me two years to persuade him to let me commission *The Wine Programme*.

Catterall: You would go out and commission these programmes. What percentage of them didn't work?

Sargant: There were four, maybe five, out of the 250 or so commissions in that eight years, that I was cross with myself about or that I had failed to have the imagination to deal with properly. None of them were complete disasters. They were broadcastable. There was one at the beginning about self-sufficiency, which should have been lovely and life-enhancing. It was one of my first experiences of going to a shoot. If I'd been a year into the job I'd have known from watching the shoot that the director was useless, and it was really dead. There was one set of children's programmes which went continually over budget.

Catterall: Wasn't there something called *Teenypops?*

Sargant: Yes, but that was Cecil Korer[18] and that came out of entertainment. That was, of course, pretty ludicrous for Channel 4. Then there were the beginnings of the ones presented by Paula Yates which were commissioned by the youth editor, and they were pretty near the knuckle.

Carol had a thing about breaking the boundaries of sex and wanting to do something on sex therapy early on. I did resist that. I remember making a joke about it. Remember my point about what happens if it works? What happens if this programme works and the guy discovers that he's a sado-masochist...

Breaking boundaries was never my goal. My goal was to try to create a space for people to do brilliant, creative things. If testing the boundaries was anyone's task it would have been Alan Fountain, say, but it wasn't the task of the educational output. Our task was to meet peoples' needs and stimulate them intellectually. I would try to be educational about things nobody else had ever thought they might be, but not by breaking taboos.

However, I did have programmes where the makers wanted to change what they wanted to do part way through. I'll give you an example from *Citizen 2000*. Documentary makers are often missionaries and zealots, with a radical message. For that series we had a regular team at Thames, but they would not necessarily commission the same programme maker each year for the annual filming. For year three they got someone who was absolutely passionate about nursery provision. She transmuted what should have been a piece of observational work following our three-year-olds into a campaigning programme about the need for nursery schools. I didn't see it until it was at fine cut stage. One then tried to de-politicise it. This was not a series which was supposed to have a campaigning edge. It was quite good that we had that out early on in the life of that series, because that made it clear to the Thames team that they needed tighter control.

The Educational Output

There were quite a lot of modest, workmanlike programmes in those 5.30pm, 6.30pm slots, which were never going to be big time. Some of the most modest were extraordinary. I told you I tried to buy programmes from each of the ITV companies, even Ulster Television. They wanted to do a series called 'Profitable Hobbies', which sounds very unpromising, and they would do it for £5,000 a programme. Amazingly cheap! It was the only one of their things that I could bear to think about, and I thought that it could go in my 'for people with more time than money' slot at 5.30pm. It covered picture-framing, jewellery-making and what have you. We changed the name to *Make It Pay* and this modest set of half-hour programmes went out at 5.30pm. It got over 1 million viewers and the accompanying booklet kept on running out.

Catterall: By the time you left in 1989 had this eclecticism narrowed and the Channel's output developed an identity, but not of this range?

Sargant: It wasn't as eclectic. When you've got more of your own repeats you get less space and less money for new programmes, and it was more difficult to do the completely off-the-wall ones like the animation. Jeremy never really closed down on it, it was more the lack of space. The last year with Jeremy in fact, he had reconstructed the internal management so that the four of us became heads of groups. We became effectively like departmental heads. David Rose was in charge of drama. I was in charge of both education and children's, and we had the Open College. Adrian Metcalf had a funny bundle, including sport, which he was very good on. And Liz Forgan had current affairs.

I'd always had the same eight-year contract as Jeremy had given himself. He always said eight years was enough. He didn't think people should have that power and also, secondly, that people couldn't go on being innovatory. I don't actually agree with that, I think some people are congenitally innovatory and others never will be. I think he was preparing for when he might leave the Channel, so therefore he was setting up a more solid structure that wasn't entirely dependent upon him. It was a time when his first wife died, and so he was essentially not playing the same active hands-on role.

I'd also been building up the children's programming to justify an individual children's commissioning editor. And increasingly we were broadcasting for longer hours and moving into the afternoon. We had a couple of attempts to work with the Manpower Services Commission and finally started doing the Open College programming at lunchtime. We bridged across through the whole day when we took over ITV for schools, which all took place still within Jeremy's time.

We had failed twice to work out something like the Open College. When I knew we were going to take over ITV schools programming and bridge across the lunchtime I wrote back to Geoffrey Holland immediately to say that this was the last occasion when there would be a large slot of time available for a potential Open College.

The children's programming was designed to be more pre-school and I bought in *Sesame Street* for these lunchtime slots. Then I had this brilliant woman programme maker who had been at Yorkshire Television, Ann Wood. She made a long series *Pob's Programme* for me over two or three years with a puppet character, Pob, living inside the television set, again aimed at the pre-school years, with activities and poems and so on. Pob became, in a way, the precursor of the *Teletubbies*, which she went on to make much later for the BBC. Neither Jeremy nor Liz liked Pob, they didn't understand children's stuff, but Pob was wonderful and the kids loved him, he became a cult. So they missed that and if they'd kept her they might have got *Teletubbies* too.

It was all still pretty open. What was sad was that Michael Grade didn't honour the educational commitment in the way that Jeremy did. He left the iconic good works – things like disability and multiculturalism – and the big audience things like gardening, but he really cut back by about 20 per cent on the rest of the educational output at the point that I went. And he waited for several months and then decided to put Liz in as the controller of the Channel. That put the rest of us further down the management line, when hitherto we'd been in complete charge of our own areas. Numbers of staff increased in a more hierarchical structure while fewer programmes were being commissioned. By and large there was also less freedom and innovation.

My classic example is that I was then commissioning an afternoon live programme three days a week from Thames, featuring Mavis Nicholson. She was a brilliant interviewer, there was a telephone helpline and so on. It was about the only thing on Channel 4 that was actually live. It was very cheap, but when Michael quite reasonably

The Educational Output

came in and looked at all our budgets for things he could change, as any new boss would, he said what's this £800,000. He had then just come back from America, where he'd apparently seen the Oprah Winfrey show, which he could buy cheaply in bulk, so he said that he wanted to cancel Mavis, and I could come and argue with him about it. I talked to Catherine Freeman at Thames, who was the provider, and we reckoned we wouldn't get anywhere if we did argue for its retention as they were both chat shows after all, with women presenters, but also Oprah was black. It gave me an insight into his strategy of doing things that look good. I was there with him for a year and never once did I have a serious conversation with Michael Grade about the educational programming, even though it was such a large part of the Channel, nor did he ever comment on any of the programmes. Education never had the pride of place that it had before.

NOTES

1. Jeremy Isaacs, *Storm Over 4*, (London: Weidenfeld & Nicolson, 1989), pp.38–9.
2. An artist who achieved fame for his imitations of Old Masters.
3. Christopher Frayling presented two Channel 4 arts series and has been Rector of the Royal College of Art since 1996.
4. Then head of features at Granada.
5. Programme Controller, Granada, 1979–87 and a Director of Channel 4 in 1984–87.
6. Managing Director of Granada, 1981–87 and Chairman of the ITV Network Programme Committee, 1980–82.
7. Director of the Institute of Education, University of London, 1973–83.
8. Channel 4's educational output is reviewed in Naomi Sargant, *Adult learners, Broadcasting and Channel 4* (London: Channel 4, 1992).
9. Peter Mennear was very helpful.
10. Member, IBA, 1980–86.
11. Jeremy Isaacs' successor as Chief Executive of Channel 4.
12. Channel 4 Commissioning Editor for Arts Programmes, 1981–89.
13. Former British ambassador to Poland, West Germany, France and the USA.
14. Senior Commissioning Editor, Channel 4, 1982–94.
15. *The World at War* consists of 26 half-hour programmes. It was first broadcast in 1974.
16. See Patrick Barwise and Andrew Ehrenberg, *Television and its Audience* (London: Sage, 1988).
17. Channel 4 Commissioning Editor, Youth, 1981–83; Senior Commissioning Editor, Entertainment, 1983–87; Controller, Arts and Entertainment and Deputy Director of Programmes, 1988–90.
18. Channel 4 Commissioning Editor, Entertainment, 1981–83.

Notes on Contributors

Peter Catterall is Director of the Institute of Contemporary British History and Visiting Lecturer in History at Queen Mary and Westfield College, London. He is currently working on a study of the British Cabinet committee system.

Edmund Dell was Labour MP for Birkenhead 1964–79 and served in the Cabinet as Secretary of State for Trade, 1976–78. He was Chairman of Guinness Peat 1979–82 and of Channel 4 1980–87. His latest book is *The Chancellors: A History of the Chancellors of the Exchequer 1945–1990* (1996).

Liz Forgan was Senior Commissioning Editor of Channel 4 in 1981–88 and its Director of Programmes 1988–93.

Shirley Littler was Assistant Under-Secretary of State in the Home Office 1978-83 and Deputy Director-General of the IBA 1986–89. Since 1992 she has been the Chairman of the Gaming Board for Great Britain.

John Ranelagh worked in Conservative Research Department 1975–79. He was a commissioning editor on Channel 4 1981–88 (and Secretary to the Board 1981–83), and Director of the Broadcasting Research Unit 1988–90. His books include *Thatcher's People* (1991).

Naomi Sargant was the commissioning editor in charge of educational and children's programmes at Channel 4, 1981–89.

Anthony Smith is President of Magdalen College, Oxford. He has

Notes on Contributors

published extensively on the media and was a member of the Channel 4 Board 1980–84.

Lord Thomson of Monifieth was Labour MP for Dundee East 1952–72. He was Chancellor of the Duchy of Lancaster 1966–67 and 1969–70, Commonwealth Secretary 1967–8 and Minister without Portfolio 1968–9. From 1973–77 he was a European Commissioner and from 1981–88 the Chairman of the Independent Broadcasting Authority.

Index

20/20 Vision, 123

adult education, 134–7, 143
adult literacy, 135, 137, 139–40
advertising, 7, 17, 55, 63, 66
   and BBC, 33, 48
   revenue, 18, 20, 27, 33–4, 37, 41, 47–8, 62, 71–4, 93, 144–6, 155
   rates, 19
Althusser, Louis, 107
American imported programmes, 10, 23, 26, 32, 82, 152
The Animals Film, 54, 81
animation, 157, 159
Annan, Lord, 43, 67, 79, 107–8
Annan Committee, ix, 1, 53, 57, 61, 66–7, 80, 92, 96, 99, 115
archaeology, 150
arts broadcasting, 7, 87, 138–9, 143, 145, 147, 156–7
Arts Council, 157
Association of Broadcasting Staff, 98
Association of Cinematograph, Television and Allied Technicians, 98
Attenborough, David, 143
Attenborough, Sir Richard, 30, 38, 40–1, 44, 93
audience research, 140, 144, 146, 154–6
audience, broadcasting, xii, xvi–xvii, 102, 145
Avila, Kay, 153

BBC1, 1, 21, 64, 154

BBC2, 2, 4, 7, 58, 64, 66, 81–83, 85
Balhatchett, Sophie, 54
Bedawi, Zeinab, 143, 150
beekeeping, 142, 156
Benedictus, David, 57
Benjamin, Floella, 150
Benn, Tony, 2
Birt, John, 5, 85, 100, 104, 105, 114, 121–22
black community, 118, 128, 131
Blake, Lord, 8, 35, 82
Bland, Christopher, 31
The Blood of the British, 149–50
Blyth, Ken, 3, 53, 55, 79, 87
Bolland, Mike, 156, 161
Bonner, Paul, 5–6, 35, 53, 79, 89, 99–100, 102, 111, 122, 142, 154
borstals, 75
Boyle, Jimmy, 99
Brazil Cinema: Sex and the Generals, 57
British Audience Research Bureau, 144, 155
British Broadcasting Corporation, xi, 4, 12, 17, 23, 47–9, 54, 60, 63–4, 66, 76–7, 84–5, 94–6, 99, 106, 135–6, 139–40, 150, 154, 160
   and Annan Committee, 115
   audience, 144–45
   competition with C4, 7, 48, 83, 87
   governors, 16
   and independent producers, 18
   licence fee, 16–17, 33, 47–8, 67, 71, 128
   management structure, 86, 95, 102

165

news coverage, 11, 128
  and Peacock Committee, 33, 48, 71
British Film Institute, 95, 100
Brittan, Leon, 65–6
Brittan, Samuel, 37
Broadcasting Act 1980, ix, 2, 21, 56, 58, 66–7, 75, 80, 82, 92–5, 146
Broadcasting Act 1990, x, 39–40, 42, 70–1, 73, 77–8, 146
broadcasting duopoly, xi, 17–18, 33, 41, 43, 48–9, 76
Broadcasting Research Unit, 83
Broadcasting Support Services, 140–1
Broadcasting White Paper 1978, 61–3, 80, 92
Broadcasting White Paper 1988, 37, 40, 49–50, 72, 82, 146
Broadside, 123
Brook Productions, 129
Brookside, 10, 32, 82, 109
Brown, Bill, 41, 53, 56, 90, 114, 125
Budd, Alan, 34–5
Buxton, Lord, 22, 44–6

Cabinet, 1–2, 61, 76, 92
cable television, ix, 32, 77
Callaghan, James, 61
Callender, Colin, 54
Capon, Susanna, 147
Central Television, 13–15, 126–7
Chapple, Frank, 13–14, 126
Chataway, Christopher, xi, 98
Channel 3 (see ITV)
Channel 4
  audience, xvi–xvii, 7, 10, 14, 32, 45, 48, 81–2, 101, 109, 125, 127, 129–30, 141, 144, 146, 154–6, 159
  Board, xvii, 2–8, 10–12, 14–15, 21–4, 27–8, 31, 34–7, 40–1, 44, 47–8, 50–1, 53–5, 65, 67–8, 70–1, 73, 78, 80–2, 85, 88–90, 94, 96–7, 100–1, 109, 112, 114, 124–5, 127, 132, 149
  Board, ITV directors on, 2, 12, 22, 31, 36, 39–41, 68, 90, 97, 124–5
  comes on air, x, 6–7, 67, 81
  commissioning, xiii, xvii–xviii, 15, 54–5, 57–8, 87, 100, 103–4, 10, 110–11, 124, 126, 128, 138–9, 142–3, 146–7, 152–4, 156–7, 159–60

commissioning budgets, 125, 138–9, 142–3, 153, 156, 159–61
commissioning editors, xviii, 6, 9, 12, 54, 57–8, 88, 102, 116, 118, 122–4, 131–2, 12, 150–1, 155, 159
controversial programmes, xvi–xvii, 11–16, 54, 56–7, 81, 105–8, 110, 115, 119, 125–7, 148–9, 158
co-ordinating committee, 15, 151
criticised, xii, xvii, 7–8, 11, 109, 127, 132, 152
editorial control, 9, 11, 15–16, 54–5, 58, 108, 119, 124, 151
established, ix, xii, 2, 80
funding regime, xvi, 2, 19–20, 26–7, 31–2, 34–5, 40–2, 47–9, 51, 55, 58, 63–7, 69, 72–4, 77, 80, 82–3, 85, 93–4, 96–7, 114, 119, 125, 128, 130, 146
hours of broadcasting, 19, 101, 137, 160
idea of, ix, xi, xvi, 1, 53, 60–5, 80, 84–5, 91–4
political balance of, 1, 6–7, 9–13, 15–16, 55, 57–9, 75, 81, 105–10, 117–19, 126, 131, 149, 151, 158
possibility of franchising, 36
possibility of privatisation, 47, 78, 146
Programme Policy Statement, 4, 24, 81–2, 84
as publisher, xix, 22–3, 80, 117–8
relations with IBA, x, xvi–xviii, 3, 8, 16–17, 19, 21–36, 47, 49–55, 57, 64, 68–71, 75–7, 82, 93, 97, 101, 111, 140
relations with independent producers, xvi, 18, 21–4, 26, 86–7
relations with ITV companies, xvi, 3, 19–26, 30–9, 41–4, 47–50, 52, 55, 57, 82, 143
remit, xii, 4, 8, 10, 23, 32, 35, 42–3, 49–51, 64–6, 69–70, 72–3, 75–6, 80–1, 87, 93, 96, 101, 103, 130, 146, 155
scheduling, 125, 129–30, 137, 143–4, 146, 151, 153–4, 157, 159
selling own advertising, x, xiii, xvii, 8, 12, 20, 27, 30–43, 46–51, 71, 78, 82, 113, 130, 144
staffing at, xiii, 32, 53, 68–9, 111, 130–1, 159–60

Index

as statutory corporation, x, 39–40, 42–3, 70, 72–3, 82
threats of legal action against, 13–14, 75
transmission coverage, 78, 155
Channel 4 News, 3, 6, 12, 21–2, 44–5, 69, 81–2, 106, 120–1, 125, 128, 138
Channel 5, 70, 72, 155
Chapman, Graham, 57
Chatham House, 16
children's broadcasting, 140, 159–60
 special needs, 147
China, 139
Chip's Comic, 147
Citizen 2000, 145, 158
citizens' juries, 107
company law, 65
Conservative Party, 9, 21, 57, 63, 69, 76, 78, 85, 92–3, 114
Conservative Research Department, 56
consumer broadcasting, 137, 141, 153
cookery on television, 141, 153
Coopers & Lybrand, 34–5
Coronation Street, 84
Couper, Heather, 150
courts, 75–6
Cox, Barry, 121
Coyne, Larry, 54
Critchley, Julian, 85, 92, 114
Crowson, Susan, 53
Crucible, 126
Cutting Edge, 155

Daily Mail, 81, 125
Day, Robin, 97
Dell, Edmund, xvii–xix, 41–3, 53, 67, 78–9, 92, 100, 103, 108, 118, 135, 149
 becomes C4 chairman, 2, 93–4, 97
 ceases to be C4 chairman, 38
 and commissioning editors, 6, 9, 12, 126
 and IBA, 8, 16–31, 34–6, 38, 40, 50–1, 54, 69–70, 75–6, 93, 97, 104, 111
 and Jeremy Isaacs, 5–9, 11, 22, 54, 59, 99, 102, 105–6, 110, 112–3
 and news and current affairs coverage, 6, 10–16, 21–2, 44–6, 58, 81, 105, 127
 owns television set, 3, 10, 105
 and Peacock Report, 27–40, 46–9, 71, 77, 82

and television, 5, 8, 10, 88–9, 105
threatens to resign, 30
Department of Education and Science, 110
Department of Industry, 63, 80
digital television, 64–5, 68, 117
Dimbleby lecture, 106
disabled, programmes for, 160
Diverse Productions, 12
Diverse Reports, 12, 57, 118
drama, on C4, 128, 155, 159
due impartiality, 8–16, 55, 62, 66, 68, 75, 105–6, 111, 131, 151
Duffy, Terry, 13–14
Dukes, Justin, 27, 35, 43, 54, 67, 79, 87, 111–2, 142

economics coverage, 6, 58, 120, 143
Eden, Sir John, 84, 114
Edinburgh Television Festival, 5, 9, 102–3, 106, 140
educational broadcasting, xviii, 32, 51, 106, 115, 143, 145, 151–3, 156, 161
 15 per cent requirement, 101, 135, 138, 141
 and adult education, 110, 136
 follow-up, 139–42
 new understanding of, 51, 136
 for older people, 137, 144, 146
 political education, 149
 pre-school, 160
 and unemployed, 137
 and women, 149–50
Ehrenberg, Andrew, 154
Eleventh Hour, 57
Ellis, John, 54
Elstein, David, 33, 85, 114, 129
engineering programming, 58
Equity, 19, 56, 68, 81, 152
Evans, Gwynfor, 21
Evans, Moss, 126

Fiddick, Peter, 98–9
film industry, 58, 83, 86, 95, 108
Film on Four, 8, 58, 111, 128
Financial Times, 6, 10, 37, 54, 105
Forgan, Liz, xviii, 15, 106, 114–5, 125–6, 138, 140, 146, 151, 156, 159–60

167

appointed, 6, 54, 88, 100, 105, 116, 142
and feminism, 122–3
freedom of action, 123–4, 126–32
and journalism, 117–123, 128, 131
lack of experience in television, 58, 116–17, 119, 121–2, 124
and television, 116–17, 120, 128, 131
workload, 118, 124, 142, 148
Fountain, Alan, 152, 158, 161
Fox, Paul, 33–4, 40, 125
Fraser, Bob, 84, 114
Frayling, Chris, 138, 161
Freeman, Catherine, 161
Freeman, John, 5, 64–5, 77
The Friday Alternative, 11–12, 81, 89,107, 120

Gallup polls, 155
Gandhi, 38
gardening programmes, 139, 141, 143, 145, 154, 160
General Elections
  1979, 21, 63, 80, 85, 93, 146
  1983, 57, 76, 131
Glencross, David, 29, 55, 58
Glentoran, David, 43
Grade, Michael, 56, 78, 131, 133, 146, 152, 160–1
Graef, Roger, 79, 85–91, 95, 105, 107
Graham, David, 12, 107
Grampian Television, 34
Granada, 16, 55, 86, 140, 143, 145
Grattan, Don, 139–40
Greece: The Hidden War, x, 11, 15, 55, 57, 81, 108, 150–1
Greenham Common, xvii, 151
Griffiths, Ellis, 53–4, 122, 142
The Guardian, ix, xii, 54, 80, 84, 98–9, 113, 116, 122–3

Hamilton, Sir James, 115
Hammond, Eric, 13–14
Harris, Anne, 54
Hart, Judith, 12
Hartog, Simon, 54
Haslam, Carol, 54, 137, 139, 142, 148–9, 151, 158
Hattersley, Roy, 56

health broadcasting, 138–9, 149
The Heart of the Dragon, 139
Heath, Edward, 92
Henderson, Sir Nicholas, 151, 161
heroin, 57
Hills, Catherine, 150
Hobday, Sir Gordon, 14
Hogg, Sarah, 121
Hoggart, Richard, 134
Holland, Geoffrey, 141, 160
Home Affairs Select Committee, 37, 49, 63, 72
Home Office, xvi, xviii, 29, 37, 61, 63, 65–7, 80, 83, 85–6
homosexuality, 57
horse racing coverage, 32
Hughes, Glyn Tegai, 53
Hurd, Douglas, 18, 36–7, 41–2, 46–7, 49, 51–2

immigration, 150
IBA, ix–xi, xvi–xviii, 3–4, 47, 53–4, 56, 60, 66–7, 69–70, 76, 82, 84, 90, 96, 100, 145
  agrees to C4 selling advertising, 39–40
  C4 as subsidiary of, 2, 20–1, 49–52, 55, 64–5, 68, 77, 80, 83, 85, 93, 97, 116, 140
  and C4's political balance, 6, 9, 14–16, 55, 57–8, 75, 106, 111, 119, 127
  and educational programming, 101, 139–41, 154–5
  guidelines on programme quotas, 23–6, 103
  and Peacock Report, 8, 20, 26–36, 71–2, 77–8
  regulatory capture, xvii, 8, 16–41
  transmission services, 19, 61–2, 64, 93
  and 1978 White Paper, 63
Independent Local Radio, ix, 67–8, 70
independent producers, xvi, 1, 15, 60, 66, 69, 80, 123, 143, 151
  expectations of C4, 94–5, 107–8, 124, 146–7
  impact of C4 on, 57, 77
  number of, 57, 86–7
  politics of, 12, 107
  relations with ITV, 39, 86, 91
  share of C4's output, 22–4, 26, 86, 91, 93, 103, 140

Index

supplying BBC and ITV, 18
IPA/Equity dispute, 19, 68, 81, 152
Incorporated Society of British Advertisers, 63, 66
ITA, ix
ITC, 39–40, 42–4, 50–1, 70–4, 78, 82, 119
ITCA, 20, 25–6, 33, 37
ITN, 3, 11, 21–3, 26, 44–6, 60, 70, 82, 106, 120–1
ITV, 45, 51–2, 57, 60, 68, 87, 91–2, 95–8, 115, 122, 147, 152
  advertising monopoly, xi, 9, 16–17, 35, 43, 47–9, 76, 89–90
  begins broadcasting, ix, 84
  complementary scheduling, 32–6, 47, 50, 62, 64, 69, 71, 90, 160
  federal system, 103–4
  franchises, 39–40, 46, 48–9, 76
  and IBA, xvii, 17–26, 30, 36, 38, 40, 65, 69
  and independent producers, 18
  industrial relations, 17, 19, 23, 26, 70, 76, 82, 90
  initial reactions to C4, 56, 64, 77
  levy to Treasury, 17–18, 43, 66–7, 82, 93
  and OBA, 63, 80
  programmes for C4, 15, 23–6, 62, 80, 103–4, 108, 126, 129, 140, 143, 145, 159
  reactions to Peacock Report, 33–7, 44, 46, 48
  selling C4's advertising, xvi–xvii, 2, 19, 23, 27, 32, 34–5, 39, 43, 46–9, 61, 63–4, 66, 80, 93–4, 112, 125, 144–6, 155
  sharing revenue with C4, 41–3, 71–2, 78
  and sponsorship, 55
  tastes catered for, xviii, 32, 50, 78, 143, 145
ITV2, xii, 1, 49–50, 60, 67, 84–6, 89, 91–2, 94–5, 98, 115
industrial relations, 17, 19, 23–6, 56, 76, 90
infotainment, 141
Inner London Education Authority, 141
In Sickness and in Health, 136
Institute of Contemporary British History, xv

IBT, 11–13, 81, 89, 105–10, 115, 125, 138, 147–50
Ireland, 99
Isaacs, Jeremy, xviii, 32, 34, 45–6, 53, 56, 67, 79, 85, 89, 97, 116–17, 133, 140, 153, 161
  and C4's audience, 10, 81, 125, 129–30
  becomes Chief Executive, 4–6, 54, 81, 105
  dominance, 58–9, 112, 131
  and educational programming, 101, 134, 136–8, 142–3, 157, 160
  leaves C4, 159
  and IBA, 8, 22–3, 26, 30, 55, 101, 103–4
  and independent producers, 57, 86, 91, 103–4
  innovation, 87, 100, 102, 124, 136–7, 139
  MacTaggart lecture, 5, 86, 95, 102, 114
  and Peacock Report, 35–6, 145–6
  programme quality and balance, 6, 8–13, 15–16, 22, 57–8, 75, 104–6, 109–10, 121, 148
  relations with C4 Board, 11–12, 15, 44, 100, 124
  relations with commissioning editors, 7, 54, 58, 100–1, 119, 124, 134, 136, 147–8, 152, 156–7
  and *Right to Reply*, 132
Storm over 4, xvii, 3, 6, 10–11, 105, 113
  supporter of ITV2, xii, 5, 91, 94, 103
  and women in television, 122
Israel, 55

Jay, Peter, 85, 114
Jenkins, Roy, 92
Jesus: The Evidence, 57
Johnson, Paul, 107
Jones, Derek, 142
Jones, Joyce, 53
Junor, Penny, 150

Keating, Tom, 138, 146–7, 161
Keen, Lesley, 157
Kenny, Mary, 81
Kensington House Group, 102, 115
Key, Robert, 101
Klee, Paul, 157

Korer, Cecil, 158, 161
Kustow, Michael, 147, 161

Labour Party, 57, 65, 80, 86, 91–3, 114, 146
Left, the, 9, 13, 57, 107–9, 148–9
Leventhal, Colin, 54
light entertainment, 154
Lind, Harold, 19
Littler review, x, 29–30, 70, 82
Littler, Shirley, xviii, 29–30, 61–7, 82, 85, 92, 111
Loach, Ken, 13–14, 126–7
London Business School, 34
London Transport, 87
London Weekend Television, 5, 31, 56, 64, 103–4, 121, 143, 154

McCall, David, 90, 114
MacDonald, Gus, 127, 140, 161
McGettigan, Frank, 54
McIntosh, Andrew, 54
McIvor, Jill, 145
McKinseys, 86–7, 102
Macmillan, Margaret, 149
Madden, Paul, 54
Make It Pay, 159
Making Sense of Economics, 143
Making Sense of Marketing, 143
Manpower Services Commission, 141, 160
marketing, 143–6, 153–5
Marxism, 107–9
Mennear, Peter, 161
mentally handicapped, programmes, 147, 155
Metcalf, Adrian, 159
Middlesex University, 143
Miller, Jonathan, 145
miners' strike 1984–85, 55, 121, 128
Ministry of Posts and Telecommunications, 84
Monopolies and Mergers Commission, 18
Montagnon, Peter, 54, 139
Montessori, Maria, 149
Morley, Peter, 84
Morris, Tony, 95
Morrison, Sara, 92, 94, 114
Mozambique, 16

Mullins, Edwin, 145
multicultural broadcasting, 147, 149, 160
Mushroom Magic, 142, 156
Musicians' Union, 56

National Consumers Council, 136
National Extension College, 136
National Film and Television Archive, 113
National Film Theatre, 85
National Front, 131
National Gas Consumers Council, 136
National Theatre, 139
nature programmes, 95, 142
The New Enlightenment, 12, 118, 120
New Right, 12, 75, 107, 110, 118
Newsam, Peter, 141
Nicholas, David, 22, 44–6, 105
Nicholson, Mavis, 160–1
Northern Ireland, 57, 61
Norwich, John Julius, 150
nuclear energy, 120
nuclear weapons, 118
numeracy programming, 136–7, 143

Offer, 17
Ofgas, 17, 76
Oftel, 17, 76
Ofwat, 17
older people, programmes for, 136–7, 144, 146
One in Five, 57
Open Broadcasting Authority, ix, xii, 1, 57, 60–2, 65, 80, 85, 93, 98, 146
Open College, 136, 143–4, 159–60
Open University, 54, 60, 62, 80, 110, 134–6, 139, 143

Palestinians, 55
Panorama, 123
Park, Andy, 54
Parliament, 20, 33, 37, 49, 64–7, 71–2, 78, 95, 103
Passage to Britain, 149–50
Peacock, Alan, 30
Peacock Committee, x, xvii, 8, 12, 21, 26, 70, 83
and BBC, 48, 71, 76
C4 evidence to, 27–9, 51

Index

and ITV levy, 18, 82
recommends C4 selling its own
  advertising, 30–41, 46–9, 71, 82, 130
Peat Marwick, 54
Pilkington Report, ix, xi, 80, 94
Pitt, Ruth, 150
Plants for Free, 141
Plowden, Lady, 2–3, 21, 27, 53, 101, 110
Plowright, David, 26, 55, 140, 161
Pob's Programme, 160
Pottery Ladies, 138, 157
poverty, 148
Pragnall, Anthony, 79, 91, 114
Preston, Peter, 98–9
prisons, 118, 120
privatisation, 118, 120
public service broadcasting, 16–17, 32, 41, 50–1, 62, 76–8, 109
Purvis, Stewart, 22, 45

Questions of Leadership, x, 11, 13–15, 81, 126–7
Quilts in Women's Lives, 157

Ranelagh, John, xvii, 53–8, 99, 115, 131, 142
regulatory capture, xvii, 8, 16–38, 55, 76
Rees, Merlyn, 61
religious broadcasting, 57, 151
Right to Reply, 22, 109, 127–9, 131–2
Robinson, Jancis, 150, 153
Rodgers, Bill, 2
Rose, David, 8, 54, 88, 100, 111, 114, 140, 142, 159
Royal College of Art, 138, 161
Royal Family, 120
Royal Opera House, 112
Royal Television Society, 31, 33, 43, 46, 63–4, 80, 114

Sargant, Naomi, xviii, 54, 115, 138, 148, 152–3, 159
  and adult education, 134–6, 139–41, 160
  appointed, 100, 134–5, 139, 142
  and consumer education, 136
  lack of experience in television, 58, 140, 142–3, 158

and feminism, 149–50
freedom of action, 139, 147, 156
and Michael Grade, 160–1
and market research, 144–5, 154–6
and television, 135, 137, 151, 158
satellite broadcasting, 32, 65, 67, 70, 72, 77
Schonfeld, Victor, 54
schools programming, 32, 51, 160
science programmes, 58, 126, 138
Scotland, 61, 129, 146
Scott, David, 54
Scott, Mike, 140, 143, 161
Scottish Health Education Council, 146
Scottish Television, 56, 114
Scum, 75–6, 111
Seabrook, Jeremy, 148
Sendall, Bernard, 114
Sesame Street, 160
Seven Up, 145
sexual politics, 56–7, 118, 158
Shaw, Colin, 55, 79, 84, 96–7, 102, 107, 109–10
Shaw, David, 33, 37, 42, 44, 56
S4C, 20–1, 39, 42, 50–1, 61–4, 66–7, 72–4, 80
Siberry Committee, 61
Sinn Féin, 57
Sizewell B, 151
Skyline, 146
Smith, Anthony, 79, 100, 107–8, 112–3
  advocates publishing channel, ix, xii, 80, 85, 96–9
  and Annan Committee, 1, 92
  and BBC, 83
  on C4 Board, 1, 3, 53, 81, 84, 94, 110
Smith, Chris, 83
Social Democratic Party, 114
Sofer, Anne, 135
South Africa, 107
sports coverage, 39, 120, 159
Starks, Michael, 96, 115
Stoessl, Sue, 154–5
structuralism, 107–8
Sunday Times, 84, 106
Swallow, Norman, 95

Take Six Cooks, 153
Taking a Line for a Walk, 157

Taylor, Sir William, 141, 161
Teenypops, 158
Teletext, 70
Teletubbies, 160
television, as medium, 5, 8, 10, 88–9, 105, 116–7, 120, 128, 131, 135, 137, 151, 158
Television Act 1954, ix
Tesler, Brian, 5, 11, 41, 53, 56, 79, 89–91, 104, 111, 125
Thames Television, 33, 49, 53–4, 96, 144–5, 153, 158, 160–1
Thatcher, Margaret, 76, 83, 92
Thatcherism, xii, 57, 113, 118
Thomas, Ward, 63
Thompson, E.P., 106–7
Thomson of Fleet, Lord, 114
Thomson of Monifieth, Lord, xviii, 17, 21–30, 35–6, 38, 54, 69, 75–7, 104, 109, 115
Top of the Pops, 128
trade unions, 13–14, 19, 23, 58, 126
Trades Unions Congress, 126
Treasury, 1–2, 17–18, 77, 83
Trident Television, 63
TSW, 104
The Tube, 128
Tusa, John, 79
TV4 Campaign, 86
TV-AM, 7, 47, 49, 68, 81, 152
TVS, 15, 108, 145, 149
Tyne Tees Television, 96, 122

Ulster Television, 159
Union World, 58
Unthinkable Committee, 114–15

video workshops, 54, 57, 152
Vorderman, Carol, 150

Wales, 20–1, 61–4, 66–7, 80
Watt, David, 16, 106
A Week in Politics, 128–9
Weekend World, 121
Wenham, Brian, 4, 43, 81, 100, 115
Wheldon, Huw, 115
Whitehead, Philip, 80
Whitehouse, Mary, 58, 75, 115
Whitelaw, William, 53, 67, 69, 96, 125
  C4's funding regime, 2, 87, 93, 97, 114
  and C4's political balance, 9, 56, 111
  and C4 remit, 64, 80, 93, 114
  and IBA, 63–5, 80, 83, 85
  and S4C, 21, 63–4
Whitney, John, 22, 26, 30, 109, 115
Wilson, Rodney, 157
The Wine Programme, 139, 153, 157
Winfrey, Oprah, 161
witness seminars, xv
Wollen, Peter, 103
women and television, 116, 122–3, 129, 140, 149–50
Wonfor, Andrea, 122
Wood, Ann, 160
Wood, David, 147
Woodford, Sue, 149
World at War, 134–5, 153
World in Action, 123
Worsley, Sir Marcus, 92, 114

Yates, Paula, 158
Years Ahead, 144–6, 151, 155
Yesterday's Men, xv, 114
Yorkshire Television, 33, 136, 143, 160
Young, Sir Brian, 2, 79, 84–6, 90–1, 93, 99, 110, 112
youth programming, 151, 158

Zamu, Ann, 115